RACQUETBALL
RULES
AND TECHNIQUES
ILLUSTRATED

RACQUETBALL ● RULES ● AND TECHNIQUES ILLUSTRATED

Edited by George Sullivan

**Produced, designed and illustrated by
Lawrence P. Konopka
and Madelon Skoogfors**

Cornerstone Library
Published by Simon & Schuster
New York

●●●●●●●●●●●●●●●●●●●●●●●●●●●●●●●●●●●

Photography by Manhattan Image, N.Y., N.Y.

*Special thanks to Miguel Aguilera, Sandra Snyder
and Racquetball Fifth Avenue, N.Y., N.Y.*

*Thanks also to John Lewis,
Kelly Griefnow and Sharon Kelly.*

Rules of Racquetball Copyright © 1982 by U.S. Racquetball Association

Copyright © 1982 by Cornerstone Library, a Simon & Schuster Division of Gulf & Western Corp.

Published by CORNERSTONE LIBRARY,
A Simon & Schuster Division of Gulf & Western Corporation

Simon & Schuster Building
1230 Avenue of the Americas
New York, New York 10020

CORNERSTONE LIBRARY and colophon are trademarks of Simon & Schuster,
registered in the U.S. Patent and Trademark Office.

10   9   8   7   6   5   4   3   2   1

Library of Congress Cataloging in Publication Data

ISBN 0-346-12564-2

Contents

Four-wall Rules

Part 1—The Game

Rule 1.1—Types of Games

Four-wall racquetball may be played by two, three, or four players. When played by two it is called singles; when played by three, cutthroat; and when played by four, doubles.

Rule 1.2—Description

Racquetball is a competitive game in which a racquet is used to serve and return a ball.

Rule 1.3—Objective

The objective is to win each rally by rally by serving or returning the ball so the opponent is unable to keep the ball in play. A rally is won when a side is unable to return the ball before it touches the floor twice.

Rule 1.4—Points and Outs

Points are scored only by the serving side when it serves an ace or wins a rally. When the serving side loses a rally, it loses the serve. Losing the serve is called a side out. Losing the first serve in doubles is a hand out.

Rule 1.5—Game

A game is won by the side first scoring 21 points.

Rule 1.6—Match

A match is won by the side first winning two games.

Rule 1.7—Tie-breaker

In the event each side wins a game, the third game will be won by the side first scoring 11 points. This 11-point third game is called a tie-breaker.

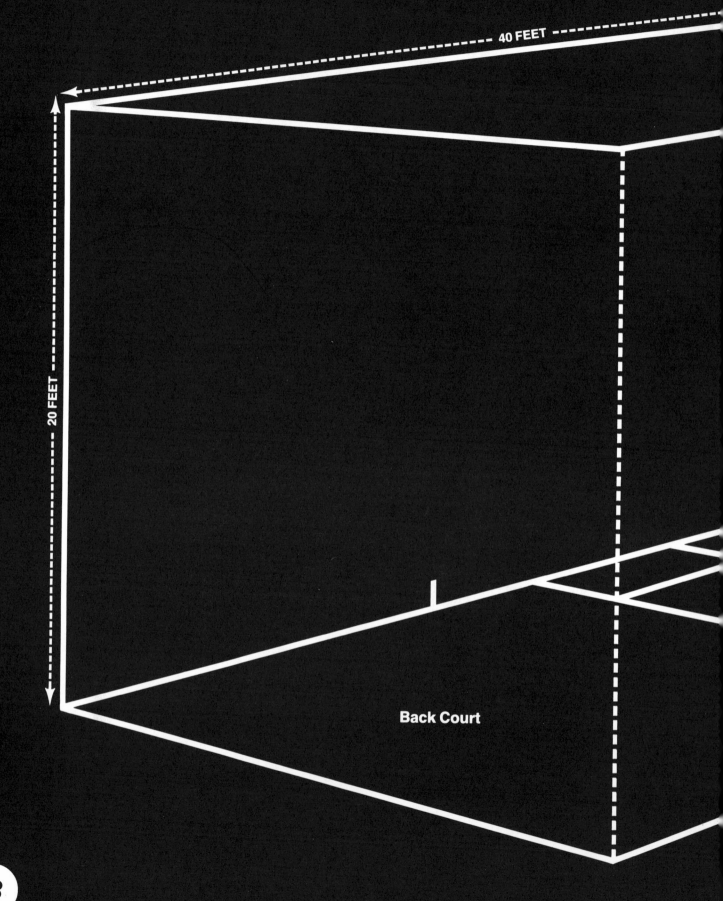

40 FEET

20 FEET

Back Court

Part 2—Court and Equipment

Rule 2.1—Court

The specifications for a standard four-wall racquetball court are:

a. Dimensions. The dimensions shall be 20 feet wide, 20 feet high, and 40 feet long, with each back wall at least 12 feet high.

b. Lines and zones. Racquetball courts shall be divided and marked on the floor with 1.5"-inch"-wide red, white, or appropriately colored lines.

1. Short line. The short line divides the court in half, parallel to the front and back walls. The back edge of the short line shall be equal distance between the front and back walls, 20 feet from both.

2. Service line. The service line is parallel with the short line, with the front edge of the service line 5 feet in front of the back edge of the short line.

3. Service zone. The service zone is the space between the outer edges of the short line.

4. The service box lines are located at each end of the service zone and designated by lines 18 inches from and parallel with each side wall.

5. Service boxes. The service boxes are the spaces between the side walls and the service-box lines.

6. Receiving lines. Five feet back of the short line, vertical lines shall be marked on each side wall extending 3 inches to 6 inches from the floor. The back edges of the receiving lines shall be 5 feet from the back edge of the short line.

Service Line

Service Zone

Service Box

Short Line

Receiving Line

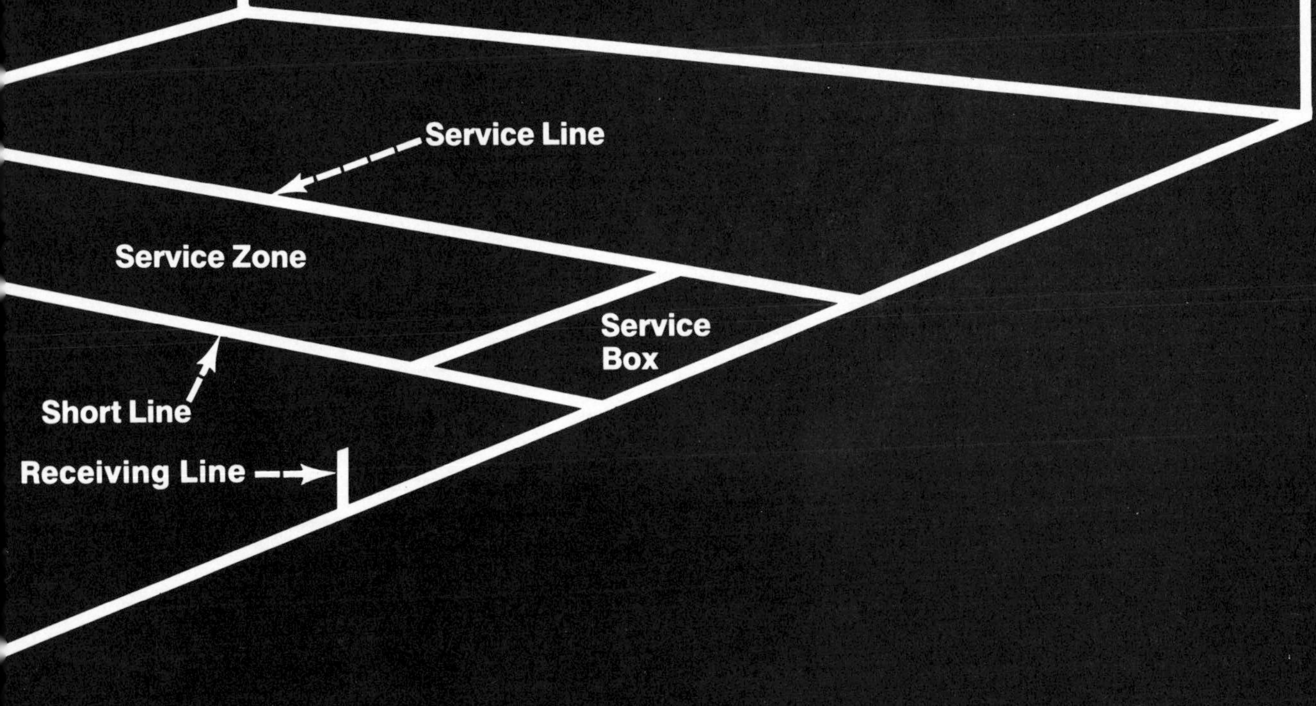

Rule 2.2—Ball specifications

The specification for the standard racquetball are:

a. Size. The ball shall be 2.25 inches in diameter.

b. Weight. The ball shall weigh approximately 1.4 ounces.

c. Bounce. The ball shall bounce 68 to 72 inches from a 100-inch drop at a temperature of 76 degrees F.

d. Official Ball. The official ball of the USRA is the blue Seamco 600; the official ball of the NRRC is the green Seamco 559; or any other racquetball deemed official by the USRA or the NRC from time to time.

Rule 2.3—Ball Selection

A ball shall be selected by the game referee for use in each match in all tournaments. During a game the referee either at his discretion, or at the request of player or team, selects another ball. Balls that are not round or that bounce erratically shall not be used.

In tournament play, the referee and the players shall agree to an alternate ball, so that in the event of breakage, the second ball can be put into play immediately.

Rule 2.4—Racquet

The official racquet shall have a maximum head length of 11 inches and a width of 9 inches. These measurements are computed from the outer edge of the racquet-head rims. The handle may not exceed 7 inches in length. Total length and width of the racquet may not exceed a total of 27 inches.

a. The racquet must include a thong, which must be securely wrapped on the players wrist.

b. The racquet frame may be made of any material, as long as it conforms to the above specifications.

c. The strings of the racquet may be gut, monofilament, nylon, or metal.

Rule 2.5—Uniform

a. General. All parts of the uniform, consisting of a shirt, shorts, socks, and shoes, should be clean. Only customary racquetball attire, in the referee's judgment, can be worn. Players may not play without shirts. Shirts must be full-length (not a shirt cut off in the torso).

b. Color. Color is optional provided, in the judgment of the referee, it does not affect the opposing player's view of the ball. (Some very dark colors or unusual patterns may do this.)

c. Wet shirts. The referee may request that a wet shirt be changed. Players should have an ample supply of dry shirts.

d. Lettering and insignia. Names of the players may appear on the back of the uniform shirts. Lettering or insignia in poor taste are not allowed.

Part 3—Officiating

Rule 3.1—Tournaments

All tournaments shall be managed by a committee or chairman, who shall designate the officials. Officials shall be approved by national or local USRA representatives.

Rule 3.2—Officials

a. A referee for all matches.

b. Two linesmen shall be appointed for all matches whenever possible, with appointed linesmen presiding over all quarterfinal, semifinal, championship, and third-place matches.

c. Additional officials, assistants, scorekeepers, or recordkeepers may be designated as desired.

Rule 3.3—Qualifications

All officials shall be experienced and trained, and shall be thoroughly familiar with these rules and with the local playing conditions. All officials must meet USRA/NRC and NRRA (National Racquetball Referees Association) or affiliates of said governing bodies qualification requirements.

Rule 3.4—Briefing

Before each match the officials and players shall be briefed on rules and on court hinders and regulations.

Rule 3.5—Referees

a. Prematch duties. Before each match commences, it shall be the duty of the referee to:

1. Be present no later than 20 minutes prior to match time for player briefing and ball selection.

2. Check on adequacy of preparation of the court with respect to cleanliness, lighting, and temperature for playability.

3. Check on availability and suitability of all materials necessary for the match such as balls, towels, scorecards, and pencils.

4. Check readiness and qualifications of assisting officials and linesmen and instruct them of their duties.

5. Point out any court hinders to the players and check to see that all equipment is in compliance with the rules.

6. Remind players to have an adequate supply of extra racquets and uniforms.

7. Introduce players, toss coin, and signal start of first game.

8. Inform the players that all rules will be carefully enforced and request any help and cooperation in calling double bounces and other infractions on the players.

b. Decisions. During games the referee shall decide all questions that may arise in accordance with these rules. In national events (that is, pro tour, regionals, national championships, national juniors, or any other event deemed "national" by the USRA or the NRC) a protest shall be decided by the USRA or the NRC national director, or in that person's absence the national commissioner, or in that person's absence the national coordinator or any other person delegated by the national director. On all questions involving judgment the decision of the referee is final. The referee shall have jurisdiction over the spectators as well as the players while a match is in progress.

c. Protests. Any decision not involving the judgment of the referee may on protest be decided by the chairman, if present, or his delegated representative.

d. Forfeitures. Any player for a singles match, or any team for a doubles match must report to play 10 minutes before the scheduled game time to avoid a forfeiture if circumstances warrant such a decision. A match may be forfeited by the referee for:

1. Unsportsmanlike conduct. Any player refusing to abide by the referee's decision or engaging in unsportsmanlike conduct.

2. Leaving the court. Any player leaving the court at a time not allowed by these rules wihout permission of the referee.

3. Failure to report. Any player for a singles match, or any team for a doubles match failing to report to play.

4. Late-start penalty. The opponent shall be awarded 1 point for each minute of delay of game up to 10 minutes. The match then shall be forfeited. This applies to the start of the match, between-game time-outs, time-outs during a game, and glove-change time-outs. Players should stay within earshot of the referee's call to help prevent the delay-of-game penalty. It is the obligation of the players to be ready to resume play on time even if the referee failed to give time warnings. If the matches are on, or ahead of, schedule, the players should be in the court warming up at least 10 minutes before the assigned match time to assure a prompt start. If running behind, the players should be dressed and ready to enter the court for a maximum 10-minute, in-court warm-up. If, for example, a player shows up five minutes late, he has restricted himself to a five-minute warm-up. The tournament chairman may permit a longer delay if circumstances warrant such a decision.

5. Failure to comply with tournament rules or policies. The match of a player or team may be forfeited by the tournament chairman or his designee for failure to obey the referee, for misconduct on the premises of the tournament between matches, or for flagrant abuse of hospitality, locker-room, or other tournament rules or procedures.

e. Technical warning. If a player's behavior is not so severe as to warrant a referee's technical, a technical warning may be issued without point deduction.

f. Referee's technical. The referee is empowered to deduct 1 point from a contestant's or his team's total score when, in the referee's sole judgment, the contestant during the course of the match is being overtly and deliberately abusive. The actual invoking of this penalty is called a referee's technical. If after the technical is called against the abusing contestant, play is not immediately continued within the alloted time provided for under the existing rules because of the action of the abusing contestant, the referee is empowered to forfeit the match in favor of the abusing contestant's opponent or opponents.

1. Profanity. Profanity is an automatic referee's technical and should be invoked by the referee whenever it occurs.

2. Excessive arguing.

3. Threats of any nature to opponents or to the referee.

4. Excessive or hard striking of the ball between rallies.

5. Excessive slamming of the racquet against walls or floor, slamming the door, or any action that might cause injury to the court or other players on the court.

6. Excessive delay.

Rule 3.6—Linesmen

Two linesmen shall be designated by the tournament chairman or referee and shall, at the referee's signal, either agree or disagree with the referee's ruling.

The official signal by a linesman to show agreement with the referee is thumbs up. The official signal to show disagreement is thumbs down. The official signal for no opinion is an open palm down. If both linesmen signal no opinion, the referee's call shall stand.

If both linesmen disagree with the referee, the referee must reverse his ruling. If one linesman agrees and one linesman disagrees or has no opinion, the referee's call shall stand. If one linesman disagrees and one linesman has no opinion, the rally shall be replayed.

Linesmen should be careful not to signal until the referee acknowledges the appeal and asks for the signal. In giving the signal, linesmen should take care not to look at each other. Any time the linesman is unsure of which call is being appealed, or what the referee's call was, he should request the referee to restate the appeal and the call.

Rule 3.7—Appeals

In any match using linesmen, a player or team may appeal certain calls by the referee. These calls are (1) kill shots (skip balls); (2) fault serves—except foot faults when called by a linesman, if linesmen are being utilized (fault serves shall include all fault serves described under Rule 4.5). (3) out serves; (4) double-bounce pickup.

The appeal must be directed to the referee, who shall then request opinions from the linesmen. Any appeal made directly to a linesman by a player or team shall be considered null and void and forfeit any appeal rights for that player for that particular rally.

a. Kill-shot appeals. If the referee makes a call of "good" on a kill-shot attempt which ends a particular rally, the loser of the rally may appeal the call if he feels the shot was not good. If the appeal is successful and the referee's original call is reversed, the player who originally lost the rally is declared winner of the rally and is entitled to every benefit under the rules—that is, point and/or service.

If the referee makes a call of "bad" or "skip" on a kill-shot attempt, he has ended the rally. The player against whom the call went has the right to appeal the call if he feels the shot was good.

If the appeal is successful and the referee's original call is reversed, the referee must then decide if the shot could have been returned had play been allowed to continue. If the shot could have been returned, or was returned, the rally shall be replayed. If the shot was a kill or pass that the opponent could not have retrieved, the player who originally lost the rally is declared winner of the rally. The referee's judgment in this matter shall be final.

b. Fault-serve appeals. If the referee makes a call of "fault" on a serve that the server felt was good, the server may appeal the call. If his appeal is successful, the server then is entitled to two additional serves. If the served ball was considered by the referee to be an ace and in his opinion there was absolutely no way for the receiver to return the serve, then a point shall be awarded to the server.

If the referee makes a "no call" on a particular serve (therefore making it a legal serve) but either player feels the serve was a fault, either player may appeal the call at the end of the rally. If the loser of the rally appeals and wins his appeal, then the situation reverts back to the point of service with the call becoming fault. If it was a first service, one more serve attempt is allowed. If the server already had one fault, the second fault would cause a side out.

c. Out-serve appeals. If the referee makes a call of "out serve," thereby stopping the play, the player against whom the call was made has the right of appeal. If his appeal is successful the referee shall revise the call to the proper call. If the referee makes no call or calls a fault but the receiver feels it was an out serve, he has the right of appeal. If his appeal is successful the serve results in a hand out.

d. Double-bounce Pickup appeals. If the referee makes a call of "two bounces," thereby stopping play, the player against whom the call was made has the right of appeal if he feels he retrieved the ball legally. If the appeal is upheld, the rally is replayed.

If the referee makes no call on a particular play during the course of a rally in which one player feels his opponent retrieved a ball on two or more bounces, the player feeling this way has the right of appeal. However, since the ball is in play, the player wishing to appeal must clearly motion the referee and linesmen by raising his nonracquet hand, thereby alerting them to the exact play which is being appealed. At the same time, the player appealing must continue to retrieve and play the rally.

If the appealing player should win the rally, no appeal is necessary. If he loses the rally, and if his appeal is upheld, the call is reversed and the "good" retrieve by his opponent becomes a double-bounce pickup, making the appealing player the winner of the rally.

Part 4—Play Regulations

Rule 4.1—Serve—Generally

a. **Order.** The player or side winning the toss becomes the first server and starts the first game. The loser of the toss shall serve first in the second game. The player or team scoring more points in games one and two combined shall serve first in the tie-breaker. In the event that both players or team score an equal number of points in the first two games, another coin toss shall be held prior to the tie-breaker with the winner of toss serving first.

b. **Start.** The serve is started from any place within the service zone. No part of either foot may extend beyond either line of the service zone. Stepping on the line (but not beyond it) is permitted. The server must remain in the service zone until the served ball passes the short line. Violations are called foot faults.

c. **Manner.** The serve is commenced by bouncing the ball to the floor while standing within the confines of the service zone and is struck by the server's racquet so that it hits the front wall and on the rebound hits the floor back of the short line, either with or without touching one of the side walls. It is permissible for the server to stand on either the service line or the short line but not beyond it.

d. **Readiness.** Serves shall not be made until the receiving side is ready, or until the referee has called the score. The referee shall take care not to call the score too soon after the previous rally. The score shall be called as both server and receiver prepare to return to their respective positions.

e. **Deliberate delays.** Deliberate delays on the part of the server or receiver exceeding 10 seconds shall result in an out or point against the offender.

1. This 10-second rule is applicable to both server and receiver, each of whom is allowed up to 10 seconds after the score has been called to serve or to be ready to receive. It is the server's responsibility to look and to be certain the receiver is ready. If the receiver is not ready, he must signal so by raising his racquet above his head. Such raising of the racquet is the only legal signal that the receiver may make to alert the referee and server that he is not ready.

2. If the server serves a ball while the receiver is signaling "not ready," the serve shall be done over with no penalty.

3. If the server looks at the receiver and the receiver is not signaling "not readiness," the server then may serve. If the receiver attempts to signal "not ready" after this point, such signal shall not be acknowledged and the serve becomes legal.

f. **Time-outs.** At no time shall a call of a time-out by a player be acknowledged by the referee if the time-out call does not precede the serve—that is, the so-called Chabot time-out is not legal. The beginning of the serve, as indicated in Rule 4.1 (c), is at the beginning of the service motion.

Rule 4.2—Serve-in Doubles

a. Server. At the beginning of each game in doubles, each side shall inform the referee of the order of service, which order shall be followed throughout the game. Only the first server serves the first time up and continues to serve first throughout the game. When the first server is out, the side is out. Thereafter both players on each side shall serve until a handout occurs.

b. Partner's position. On each serve, the server's partner shall stand erect with his back to the side wall and with both feet on the floor within the service box until the served ball passes the short line. Violations are called foot faults subject to the penalties therefor.

Rule 4.3—Defective Serves

Defective serves are of three types, resulting in penalties as follows:

a. Dead-ball serve. A dead-ball serve results in no penalty and the server is given another serve without canceling a prior illegal serve.

b. Fault serve. Two fault serves result in a hand out or a side out.

c. Out serves. An out serve results in a hand out or a side out.

Rule 4.4—Dead-ball Serves

Dead-ball serves do not cancel any previous illegal serve. They occur when an otherwise legal serve:

a. Hits the partner. Hits the server's partner on the fly on the rebound from the front wall while the server's partner is in the service box. Any serve that touches the floor before hitting the partner in the box is a short.

b. Is a screen ball. Passes too close to the server or the server's partner to obstruct the view of the returning side. Any serve passing behind the server's partner and the side wall is an automatic screen.

c. Is a court hinder. If in the referee's opinion an erratic bounce caused by a court obstruction affected play, it should be called a court hinder. The player should not stop play at any time in anticipation of a call, nor influence the call.

Included in court hinders is an unplayable, wet, skidding ball that has hit a wet spot on the floor. This is the referee's, not the player's call.

d. Involves a broken or a defective ball. A serve during which the ball breaks is a dead-ball serve.

Rule 4.5—Fault Serves

The following serves are faults, and any two in succession result in a hand out or a side out.

a. Foot faults. A foot fault results when:

1. The server does not begin his service motion with both feet in the service zone, and he remains within the service zone until the ball passes the short line. Standing on but not over the lines is permitted. Violations are called foot faults.

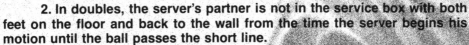

2. In doubles, the server's partner is not in the service box with both feet on the floor and back to the wall from the time the server begins his motion until the ball passes the short line.

b. Short service. A short service is any served ball that first hits the front wall and on the rebound hits the floor in front of the back edge of the short line either with or without touching one side wall.

c. Three-wall serve. A three-wall serve is any ball served that first hits two side walls on the fly.

d. Ceiling serve. A ceiling serve is any served ball that touches the ceiling after hitting the front wall either with or without touching one side wall.

e. Long serve. A long serve is any served ball that first hits the front wall and rebounds to the back wall before touching the floor.

f. Out-of-court serve. Any ball going out of the court on the serve is an out-of-court serve.

Rule 4.6—Out Serves

Any one of the following serves results in a hand out or a side out. The server must be within the boundaries described as the service zone when the serve is commenced.

a. Missed ball. Any attempt to strike the ball on the first bounce that results either in a total miss or in touching any part of the server's body other than his racquet.

b. Nonfront serve. Any served ball that strikes the server's partner, or the ceiling, floor, or side wall before striking the front wall.

c. Touched serve. Any served ball that on the rebound from the front wall touches the server on the fly or touches the server's partner while any part of his body is out of the service box or the server's partner intentionally catches the served ball on the fly.

d. Out-of-order serve. In doubles, when either partner serves out of order.

e. Crotch serve. If the served ball hits the crotch of the front wall and floor, or the front wall and side wall, it is an out serve. Any crotch serve into the back wall (or side wall on three-wall serves) is good and in play.

Rule 4.7—Return of Serve

a. Receiver or receivers. The receiver or receivers may not infringe on the receiving lines until the ball has either bounced beyond the short line or passed the receiving lines. Therefore, the receiver or receivers may not execute a fly return within the 5-foot safety zone. Violation by the receiver or receivers results in a point for the server.

b. Defective serve. To eliminate any misunderstanding, the receiving side should not catch or touch a defectively served ball until called by the referee or until it has touched the floor the second time.

c. Fly return. In making a fly return it is illegal to strike the return of serve on the fly in front of the receiver's 5-foot restraining line. After the server has struck the ball the receiver may cross the 5-foot line to return the serve if the ball bounces between the short line and the receiving line. If the ball does not bounce, the receiver cannot hit it. Any serve that passes the 5-foot line in the air may be returned on the fly. Violation by the receiver results in a point for the server.

d. **Legal return.** After the ball is legally served, one of the players on the receiving side must strike the ball with his racquet either on the fly or after the first bounce and before the ball touches the floor the second time to return the ball to the front wall either directly or after touching one or both side walls, the back wall, or the ceiling, or any combination of those surfaces. A returned ball may not touch the floor before touching the front wall (1) if it is legal to return the ball by striking the ball into the back wall first, then hitting the front wall on the fly or after hitting the side wall or ceiling; (2) if the ball should strike the front wall, then the back wall and then the front wall again without striking the floor—the player whose turn it is to strike the ball may do so by letting the ball bounce after hitting the front wall a second time; (3) if the ball strikes the front wall, then the back wall, and then the front wall again after striking the floor—the player whose turn it is to strike the ball must do so by striking it before it hits the floor a second time.

e. **Failure to return.** The failure to return a serve results in a point for the server.

Rule 4.8—Changes of Serve

a. **Hand out or side out.** A server is entitled to continue serving until:

1. **Out serve.** He makes an out serve under Rule 4.6, or

2. **Fault serve.** He makes two fault serves in succession under Rule 4.5, or

3. **Hits partner.** He hits his partner with an attempted return, or

4. **Return failure.** He or his partner fails to keep the ball in play by returning it as required by Rule 4.7 (d), or

5. **Avoidable hinder.** He or his partner commits an avoidable hinder under Rule 4.11.

6. Violation of the 10-second rule as stated in Rule 4.1 (e).

b. **Side out.** (1) **In singles.** In singles, retiring the server retires the side. (2) **In doubles.** In doubles, the side is retired when both partners have been put out, except on the first serve as provided in Rule 4.2 (a).

c. **Effect.** When the server or the side loses the serve, the server or serving side shall become the receiver; and the receiver or receiving side, the server; and so alternatively in all subsequent services of the game.

Rule 4.9—Rallies

Each legal return after the serve is called a rally. Play during rallies shall be according to the following rules:

a. **Legal hits.** Only the head of the racquet may be used at any time to return the ball. The ball must be hit with the racquet in one or both hands.

Switching hands to hit a ball is an out. The use of any portion of the body to hit the ball and "carrying" the ball on the face of the racquet are illegal hits and result in the loss of the rally.

b. One touch. In attempting returns, the ball may be touched only once by one player on the returning side. In doubles, both partners may swing at the ball, but only one may hit the ball. Each violation of (a) or (b) results in a hand out or point.

c. Return attempts.

1. In singles. In singles, if a player swings at but misses the ball in play, the player may repeat his attempts to return the ball until it touches the floor the second time.

2. In doubles. In doubles, if one player swings at but misses the ball, both he and his partner may make further attempts to return the ball until it touches the floor the second time. Both partners on a side are entitled to an attempt to return the ball.

3. Hinders. In singles or doubles, if a player swings at but misses the ball in play and in his or his partner's attempt again to play the ball there is an unintentional interference by an opponent, it shall be a hinder. (See Rule 4.10.)

d. Touching the ball. Except as provided in Rule 4.10 (a) (2), any touching of a ball before it touches the floor the second time by a player other than the one making a return is a point or out against the offending player.

e. Out-of-court ball.

1. After return. Any ball returned to the front wall which on the rebound or on the first bounce goes into the gallery or through any opening in a side wall shall be declared dead and the serve replayed.

2. No return. Any ball not returned to the front wall, but which caroms off a player's racquet into the gallery or into any opening in a side wall either with or without touching the ceiling, side, or back wall shall be an out or point against the player or players failing to make the return.

f. Dry ball. During the game and particularly on service every effort should be made to keep the ball dry. Deliberate wetting shall result in an out.

g. Broken ball. If there is any suspicion that the ball has broken during the serve, or during a rally, play shall continue until the end of the rally. The referee or any player may request that the ball be examined. If the referee decides the ball is broken or otherwise defective, a new ball shall be put into play and the rally replayed.

h. Ball inspection. The ball may be inspected by the referee between rallies at any time during a match.

i. Play stoppage. (1) If a player loses a shoe or other equipment, or if foreign objects enter the court, or if any other outside interference occurs, the referee shall stop the play. (2) Players wearing protective eyeglasses have the responsibility of having such eyeglasses securely fastened. In the event that such protective eyeglasses should become unfastened and enter the court, the play shall be stopped if such eyeglasses were fastened initially. In the event such eyeglasses were not securely fastened initially no stoppage of play shall result and the player wearing such eyeglasses plays at his own risk. (3) If a player loses control of his racquet, time should be called after the point has been decided, providing the racquet does not strike an opponent or interfere with ensuing play.

Rule 4.10—Dead-ball hinders

Hinders are of two types—dead-ball hinders and avoidable hinders. Dead-ball hinders as described in this rule result in the rally being replayed. Avoidable hinders are described in Rule 4.11.

a. Situations. When called by the referee, the following are dead-ball hinders:

1. Court hinders. A ball that hits any part of the court which under local rules is a dead ball.

2. Hitting an opponent. Any returned ball that touches an opponent on the fly before it returns to the front wall. The player who has been hit or nicked by the ball may call this hinder but must call it immediately.

3. Body contact. Body contact is not automatically a hinder and it will be the referee's decision to allow play to continue if, in his judgment, the contact did not severely interrupt the flow of play.

4. Screen ball. Any ball rebounding from the front wall close to the body of a player on the side which just returned the ball to interfere with or prevent the returning side from seeing the ball. See Rule 4.4 (b).

5. Straddle ball. A ball passing between the legs of a player on the side which just returned the ball if there is no fair chance to see or return the ball.

6. Backswing hinder. If there is body contact on the backswing the player must call it immediately.

7. Other interference. Any other unintentional interference which prevents an opponent from having a fair chance to see or return the ball.

b. Effect. A call by the referee of a hinder stops the play and voids any situation following, such as the ball hitting a player. No player is authorized to call a hinder, except on the backswing or when a player is hit or nicked by the ball, and such a call must be made immediately as provided in Rule 4.10 (a), (2) and (6).

c. Avoidance. While making an attempt to return the ball, a player is entitled to a fair chance to see and return the ball. It is the duty of the side that has just served or returned the ball to move so that the receiving side may go straight to the ball and not be required to go around an opponent. In the judgment of the referee, on the other hand, the receiver must make a reasonable effort to move toward the ball.

d. In doubles. In doubles, both players on a side are entitled to a fair and unobstructed chance at the ball, and either one is entitled to a hinder even though naturally it would be his partner's ball and even though his partner may have attempted to play the ball or may already have missed it. It is not a hinder when one player hinders his partner.

Rule 4.11—Avoidable Hinders

1. View obstruction. Deliberately moving across a player's line of vision just before he strikes the ball.

2. Distraction. Any avoidable intimidation or distraction that would interfere with the player playing the ball such as stomping feet, shouting, whistling, or other loud noise.

3. Failure to move. Does not move sufficiently to allow an opponent his shot.

4. Blocking. Moves into a position effecting a block on the opponent about to return the ball or, in doubles, one partner moves in front of an opponent as his partner is returning the ball.

5. Moving into the ball. Moves in the way of and is struck by the ball just played by his opponent.

6. Pushing. Deliberately pushing or shoving an opponent during a rally.

Rule 4.12—Rest Periods

a. Time-outs. During a game each player in singles, or each side in doubles, either while serving or receiving, may request a time-out. Each time-out shall not exceed 30 seconds. No more than three time-outs in a game shall be granted each singles player or each team in doubles. Two time-outs shall be allotted each player in singles or each team in doubles in the tie-breaker.

1. Equipment time-out. At the discretion of the referee, equipment time-outs may be granted for lost shoes, broken shoelaces, torn equipment, wet shirts, wet floor, etc. A player is not charged for such a time-out.

b. Injury. If a player is injured during the course of a match as a result of contact with the ball, racquet, opponent, wall, or floor, he shall be granted an injury time-out. An injured player shall not be allowed more than a total of 15 minutes of rest. If the injured player is not able to resume play after total rest of 15 minutes, the match shall be awarded to the opponent or opponents. On any further injury to the same player the tournament director or his designee shall determine whether the injured player shall be allowed to continue. Muscle cramps and pulls, fatigue, and other ailments that are not caused by direct injury on the court shall not be considered as injuries.

c. Between games. A 5-minute rest period is allowed between the first and second games, and a 5-minute rest period is allowed between the second and third games. Players may leave the court between games but must be on the court and ready to play at the expiration of the rest period.

d. Postponed games. Any games postponed by the referee due to weather elements shall be resumed with the same score as when postponed.

Part 5—Tournaments

Rule 5.1—Draws

The seeding method of drawing shall be the standard method approved by the USRA and the NRC. All draws in professional brackets shall be the responsibility of the national director of the NRC.

Rule 5.2—Scheduling

a. Preliminary matches. If one or more contestants are entered in both singles and doubles they may be required to play both singles and doubles on the same day or night, with little rest between matches. This is a risk assumed on entering both singles and doubles. If possible the schedule should provide at least an hour rest period between all matches.

b. Final matches. Where one or more players have reached the finals in both singles and doubles, it is recommended that the doubles match be played on the day preceding the singles match. This would assume more rest between the final matches. If both final matches must be played on the same day or night, the following procedure should be followed:

1. The singles match be played first.

2. A rest period of not less than AN HOUR be allowed between the finals in singles and doubles.

Rule 5.3—Notice of Matches

After the first round of matches it is the responsibility of each player to check the posted schedules to determine the time and place of each subsequent match. If any change is made in the schedule after posting, it shall be the duty of the committee or chairman to notify the players of the change.

Rule 5.4—Third Place

In championship, national, state, district, etc., tournaments, if there is a playoff for third place, the loser in the semifinals must play for third place or lose his ranking for the following year unless he is unable to compete because of injury or illness. See Rule 3.5 (d) (4). In all USRA/NRC-sanctioned events, the tournament director or a USRA/NRC affiliate can elect to award a semifinalists award in lieu of a third-place playoff.

Rule 5.5—USRA Regional Tournaments

Each year the United States and Canada are divided into regions for the purpose of sectional competition preceding the national championships. The exact boundaries of each region are dependent on the location of the regional tournaments. The locations are announced in *National Racquetball* magazine.

a. Only players residing in the area defined can participate in a local tournament.

b. Winners of open singles and ladies' open singles in regional tournaments will receive round-trip air-coach tickets to the USRA national tourney. Remuneration will be made after arrival at the nationals.

c. A USRA officer will be in attendance at each regional tournament and will coordinate activities with the host chairman.

Tournament Management

In all USRA-sanctioned tournaments the tournament chairman and/or the national USRA officials in attendance may decide on a change of courts after the completion of any tournament game if such a change will accommodate better spectator conditions.

Tournament Conduct

In all USRA-sanctioned tournaments the referee is empowered to default a match if an individual player or team conducts itself to the detriment of the tournament and the game.

Professional Definition

Any player who has accepted one thousand dollars or more in prize money (this amount relates only to the NRC tour) cannot participate in USRA amateur tournaments.

Age Brackets

The following age brackets, determined by the age of the player on the first day of the tournament, are:

- Men amateur singles open: any age
- Men veteran open: over thirty
- Men senior singles: over thirty-five
- Men veteran senior singles: over forty
- Men masters singles: over forty-five
- Men veteran masters singles: over fifty
- Men golden masters singles: over fifty-five
- Men veteran golden masters singles: over sixty
- Women amateur singles open: any age
- Women veteran open: over thirty
- Women senior singles: over thirty-five
- Women veteran singles: over forty
- Women masters singles: over forty-five
- Women veteran master singles: over fifty
- Juniors—separate events for boys and girls:
    Ten and under
    Twelve and under
    Fifteen and under
    Seventeen and under

One-wall Rules

At the first national one-wall championships in 1980, the following rules applied:

One-wall racquetball is played on a court with a front wall 20 feet wide and 16 feet high, including any top line. The floor is 20 feet wide and 34 feet from the wall to the back edge of the long line. There is a minimum of 6 feet beyond the long line and 6 feet outside each side line to permit the players to move. The short line is 16 feet from the back edge of the front wall to the outside edge of the 1½-inch short line. Service markers are at least 6 inches long parallel to and midway between the long and short lines, extending in from the side lines.

All four-wall rules apply, with the following exceptions:

a. One serve only is allowed.

b. Any serve landing out of bounds (side line or back line) is an automatic side out.

c. The server either (1) stands to the left or right of center and serves to the wider (more open) portion of the court or (2) stands in the center and designates to which side he or she is serving.

d. Any serve that passes within 18 inches of the server's body is a fault and a side out.

e. In doubles the server who isn't serving must stand off the court to the side either at the serving line or behind the back line.

f. The referee who calls the score is located behind the back line. The linesman is located to the right of the short line.

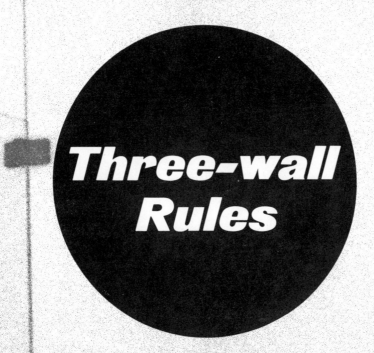

Three-wall Rules

Three-wall racquetball is played on courts with:

a. A front wall and two side walls (no back wall).

b. Front wall, a back wall, and one side wall (one side open)—a jai-alai-type court.

While there are no standard dimensions (some courts are 24 feet wide, 48 feet long, 24 feet high; others are 22 feet wide, 44 feet long, 22 feet high, etc.), the standard 20-foot-wide, 40-foot-long, and 20-foot-high court is recommended.

Three-wall racquetball (no back wall)

Regardless of the dimensions, the court should be divided into a front and back court of equal dimensions by a line called the short line, running parallel with the front wall.

From the outer edge of each side wall and running parallel with the front wall, a line should be drawn known as the long line (back-court boundary line).

Other floor markings, service line, service box (where partner stands), etc.—should be the same as those for four-wall courts.

The playing rules for games on the three-wall courts are the same as those for the four-wall game with the exception that a ball, in play, striking outside the long line is a point, or side out (or hand out), as the case may be. A service ball striking outside the long line is a long ball. Two long balls in succession, or one long and one short ball put the server out.

Three-wall Racquetball (jai-alai-type court)

The jai-alai-type court game brings into play all the skills required in making back-wall, side-wall, and corner shots common to four-wall play, and with the open-side play requires the accuracy and well-controlled shots of one-wall racquetball.

The jai-alai court has the same dimensions and playing area as the standard four-wall court—20 feet wide, 40 feet long, 20 feet high. A 1½-inch line called the outside line is drawn on the open side of the court from the front to the back wall. Balls striking outside this line are points or side outs (or hand outs), as the case may be.

The floor markings: short line service line, service box, etc., are the same as for a four-wall court, with the short line dividing the court into equal dimensions. The front wall for the first game is used as the back wall for the next game; the players simply change court serving ends after each game. This eliminates any unfair advantage a player having a strong right hand or left hand may have over a player with a weak left or right hand.

The present four-wall s racquetball rules apply: service, shorts, or longs, foot faults, receiving, hinders, etc.; the one-wall rules apply to all balls striking outside the side line.

For further information write to the Recreation and Cultural Affairs Administration, 830 Fifth Avenue, New York, NY 10021.

Racquetball Techniques

Chapter 1
Getting Started

Racquetball is a game played on a four-wall handball court in which the basic rules of handball apply, except that a short-handled strung racket is used in striking a slightly larger and softer ball. It combines the strokes of tennis with the fast pace and excitement of handball.

The game mushroomed in popularity during the 1970s. At the beginning of the decade, there were 75,000 players. By 1980, there were 7.7 million, and some estimates said the number was closer to 12 million.

Racquetball attracts players because it is so easy to learn. The object is to strike the ball so that your opponent is unable to return it successfully to the front wall. Points can be scored only by the server. The first person to score 21 points wins. A game takes only 20 to 30 minutes.

Equipment

A regulation ball is just under 2 inches in diameter and weighs a little less than 1.5 ounces. Seamco, Ektelon, and Voit are some of the leading brands. The chief requirement of the ball is that it be "live." At room temperature, when dropped from a height of 100 inches, the ball should rebound to a height of from 68 to 72 inches.

You can spend anywhere from ten to fifty dollars for a racquet. However much you spend, be sure the handle is the right size for your hand. Try this test: Grasp the racquet with only your middle and fourth fingers, circling them around the handle so the tips

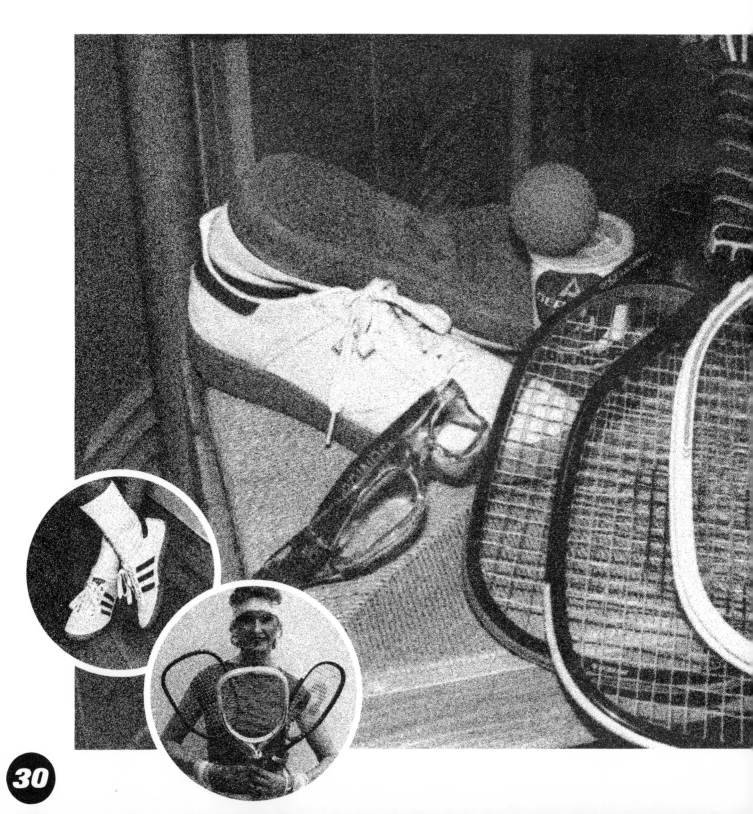

touch your thumb. You then should be able to hit the ball without the racquet twisting or turning.

The racquet handle cannot exceed 7 inches in length. The head cannot be more than 11 inches long and 9 inches wide. Even if you have a small hand, you'll find

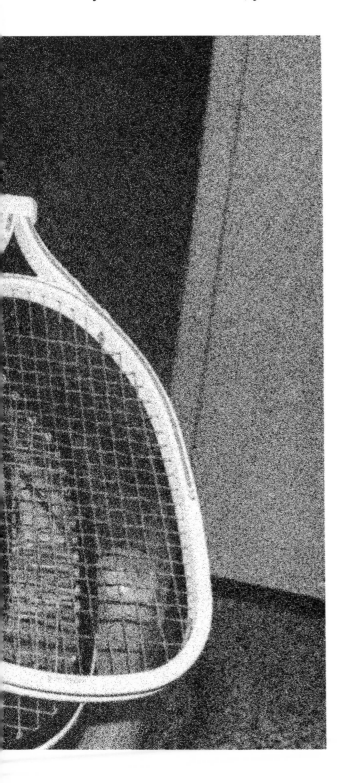

the racquet is a cinch to control (providing the handle is the right size).

Racquet frames are made of wood, aluminum, fiberglass, or graphite, or a combination of two or more of these. Fiberglass absorbs more of the ball's impact, which makes the game easier on your hand and arm. Aluminum and graphite are the most durable. Racquets vary from 230 to 245 grams in weight.

Racquets also vary as to the amount of stiffness they have. A beginner usually does his or her best with a racquet of at least moderate stiffness. Most intermediate to advanced players seek flexibility.

No matter what type of racquet you select, it will be fitted with a leather thong at the handle's butt end. Be sure to loop the thong around your wrist whenever you take the court. This prevents the racquet from flying out of your hand and striking another player.

Eyewear is vital. Indeed, in Canada the wearing of eye protection is mandatory by law, and some U.S. states have such legislation under consideration. The speed of the ball and the frequency of collisions are constant hazards to unprotected eyes.

Eyewear takes the form of stylish spectacles or wraparound goggles held in place by a head strap. For those who wear eyeglasses, eyewear with prescription lenses is available.

Although special racquetball fashions now are available, they are by no means mandatory. Just be certain that the shorts and top you wear are white or light in color. Against dark green, dark blue, or black clothing, the ball can be difficult to see. Cotton absorbs perspiration better than and keeps you cooler than synthetic fabrics.

Once you've decided to take up the sport seriously, get a pair of racquetball shoes. They have the deep treads of basketball shoes for sure footing, but they are lighter in weight. Tennis shoes are adequate until you get racquetball shoes.

Etiquette and Safety

Racquetball is a fast-moving, aggressive game played in a confined space by two racquet-swinging individuals, each bent on controlling a certain area of the court. Bruises, welts, and even more serious injuries sometimes can result.

Control your swing. *Never* swing if there is any chance of hitting your opponent.

Allow your opponent to execute his

swing and his follow-through. If you should get hit by your opponent's racquet, it's your fault. It's up to you to keep your distance.

Whenever your opponent is positioned behind you, move far enough to the right or left to allow him a "hitting alley" to the front wall. If you stand in this lane during official tournament competition, the referee may charge you with an "avoidable hinder," whether or not the ball hits you. In such cases, the point or serve goes to your opponent.

Always allow your opponent access to the ball. You also can be charged with an avoidable hinder if you fail in to execute his swing.

Chapter 2
The Forehand Stroke

The forehand stroke is the game's most important stroke. You can play about two thirds of the court with the forehand and it is the stroke you use virtually every time you serve.

To achieve a forehand stroke that's powerful and accurate, you must develop a decisive wrist snap. If you swing with a firm wrist, as in tennis, your forehand will be weak and ineffective; you'll only be tapping the ball.

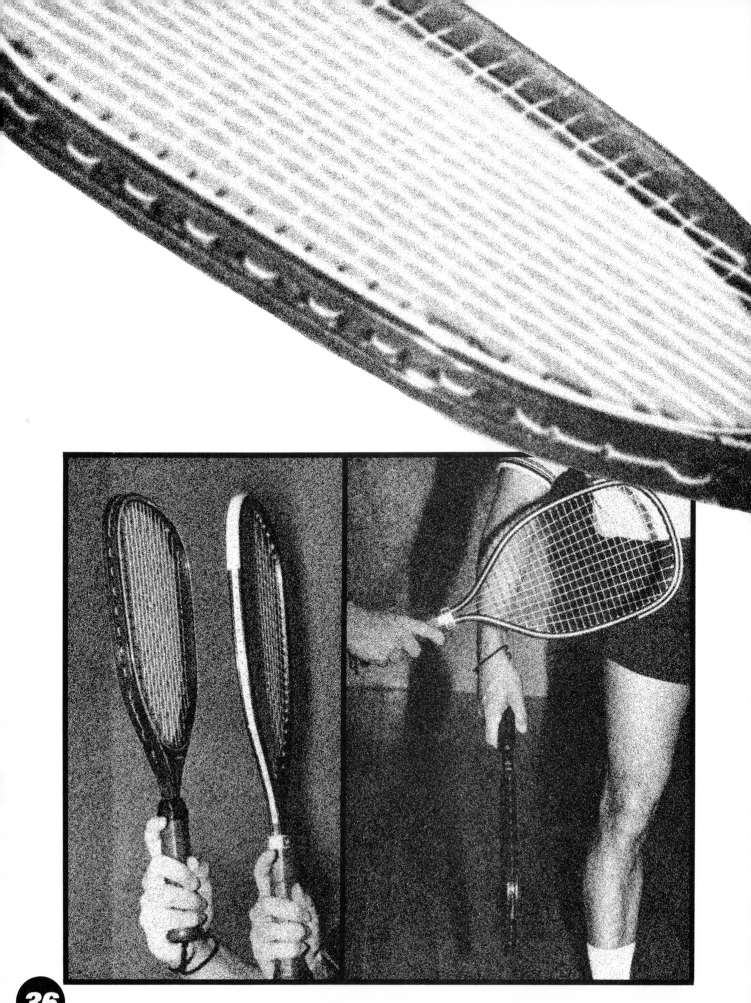

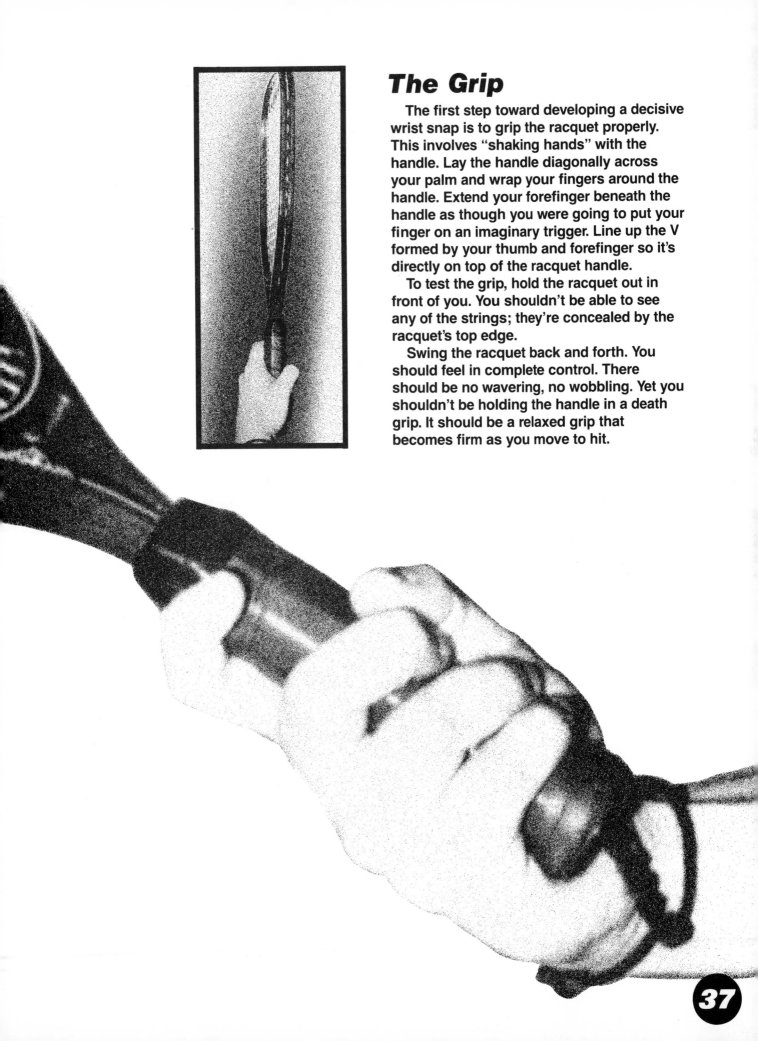

The Grip

The first step toward developing a decisive wrist snap is to grip the racquet properly. This involves "shaking hands" with the handle. Lay the handle diagonally across your palm and wrap your fingers around the handle. Extend your forefinger beneath the handle as though you were going to put your finger on an imaginary trigger. Line up the V formed by your thumb and forefinger so it's directly on top of the racquet handle.

To test the grip, hold the racquet out in front of you. You shouldn't be able to see any of the strings; they're concealed by the racquet's top edge.

Swing the racquet back and forth. You should feel in complete control. There should be no wavering, no wobbling. Yet you shouldn't be holding the handle in a death grip. It should be a relaxed grip that becomes firm as you move to hit.

Cocking and Snapping the Wrist

Let's assume that your opponent's shot is going to allow you to turn your body so your nonhitting shoulder is facing the front wall. Begin the stroke by getting the racquet up to the level of your head, then cock your wrist. That means you should bend the racquet back slightly so it can be snapped forward as you make contact with the ball.

The Stroke

Plant your right foot and begin stepping forward with your left. At the same time, move your elbow down and into the ball. The racquet head should remain in its cocked position.

As your arm straightens, contact the ball off the front foot, snapping the wrist forward and whipping the racquet through.

Your goal should be for the ball to travel into the front wall at the same height, or lower than it arrived. Be sure to keep your eyes on the ball before, during, and after the stroke.

The Follow-through

The follow-through should come naturally. The racquet head should end up behind your left ear, with the wrist fully snapped. From beginning to end, your body should be in good balance.

Practice the forehand stroke, striving for a smooth, continuous motion. Once you've achieved this flow, work on hitting the ball harder and harder. You should be able to increase the power of the stoke without great effort.

Remember, you shouldn't be stroking merely with your arm and shoulder in an effort to achieve power. Instead, try to imagine the swing actually beginning in the legs, traveling upward into your body and shoulders and down through your hitting arm. When you make contact, the wrist snap releases the built-up power.

Once you feel you've achieved a smooth and powerful stroke, work on accuracy. Put several pieces of tape on the wall and use them as targets. Keep stroking until you can hit them with some consistency.

A key factor toward achieving success is driving the ball on a straight line as close to

Getting Low to the Ball.

the floor as possible. Part of every practice session should be spent in getting low to the ball while maintaining a level swing.

The most efficient way of doing this is to move to he ball with the knees bent, then staying low or dropping lower as you whip the racquet through. But this is difficult; most people prefer to move from an upright position. An alternative method is to drop your hitting shoulder as the swing begins. At the same time, tuck your elbow to your side.

Try it; notice how you can swing the racquet through on an arc that's both low and flat.

You don't want to swing down at the ball fron an upright position. It's likely the ball either will soar high into the front wall or be driven into the floor for a "skip."

To practice keeping the ball low, place a strip of tape on the front wall 3 feet from the floor. As you take your practice shots, keep the ball between the tape and the floor. When you're able to do this consistently, lower the tape another 6 inches and repeat the drill.

Also practice the forehand under simulated game conditions. Hit the ball into the front wall as it rebounds toward you with an easy bounce. Have your racquet set, step into the ball, and drive home a front-wall winner. Work on timing, placement, and a smooth stroke. When the kill attempt goes awry and the ball rebounds high into the air, try "rekilling" it.

Chapter 3
The Backhand Stroke

Even among skilled and experienced players, a strong, reliable backhand is something of a rarity. If you can develop this stroke, hitting the ball authoritatively, keeping it low, you'll be a giant step ahead of most of your opponents.

The problem in executing the backhand stroke is that it feels awkward. The forehand is a much more natural stroke. All you have to do is step into the ball and snap your wrist, and you'll still be able to hit hard. But with the backhand, you have to turn your body around and then swing through, snapping your wrist. Given sufficient time, most people can get into position and hit a backhand, but the result invariably is a feeble shot.

With practice, however, the backhand can be made to feel natural, it can come to equal the forehand in terms of both power and accuracy. It's simply a matter of learning the fundamentals, then practicing.

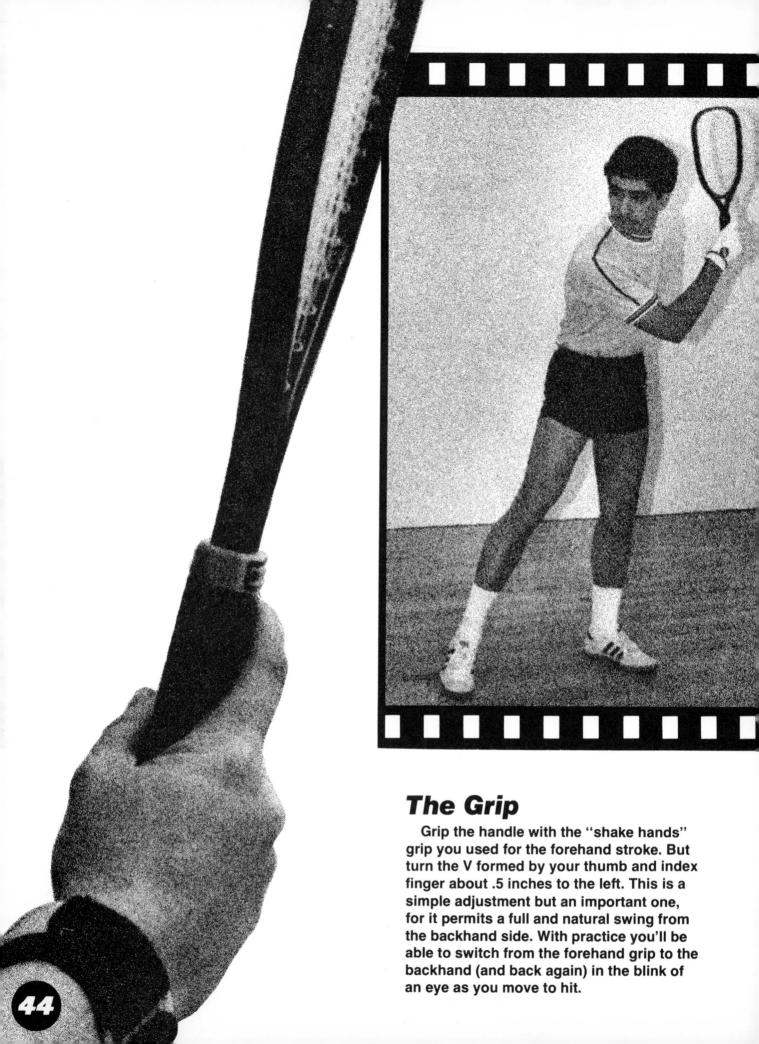

The Grip

Grip the handle with the "shake hands" grip you used for the forehand stroke. But turn the V formed by your thumb and index finger about .5 inches to the left. This is a simple adjustment but an important one, for it permits a full and natural swing from the backhand side. With practice you'll be able to switch from the forehand grip to the backhand (and back again) in the blink of an eye as you move to hit.

Cocking Your Wrist

As you get set to hit the ball, your body should be facing the side wall. Turn your shoulders so they are facing the back wall.

At the same time, pull the racquet back, bending the hitting arm and tilting your wrist back.

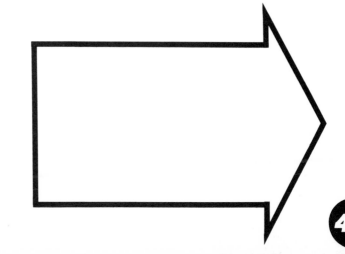

The Full Body Swing

As you step with the right foot and start the arm forward, keep the racquet back and your wrist cocked. Just before contact, the right arm straightens and the wrist starts to break. Your point of contact with the ball should be directly in front of the lead foot.

Keep your wrist firm after it has snapped through. This prevents the racquet head from rolling over, which can drive your shot into the floor.

Be sure to follow through, keeping your swing as level as possible. Too high a follow-through will send the ball to a point high on the front wall. A level-swing follow-through should result in a level shot.

Most people have problems with the backstroke because they fail to take a full swing. They merely punch the ball. Bear this in mind during your practice sessions. Wind up and really tee off. Don't be con-

cerned about where the ball is going to go.
Once you've developed a healthy swing,
you can start to worry about accuracy.

Use the same practice drills as outlined
for the forehand stroke. Drop the ball to the
floor and hit the rebound from the backhand side. Work on an assortment of shots.

Try hitting backhands to the front wall so
the return goes to your backhand side, en-
abling you to execute a backhand kill. If
you have difficulty hitting a backhand to
your backhand side, begin the drill with a
forehand lob; then circle around and
smash a backhand.

When you feel you've gained some facil-
ity with the stroke, practice hitting at a
lower contact point to get the ball lower.
Try hitting the ball into the left wall, keeping
it within 3 feet of the floor.

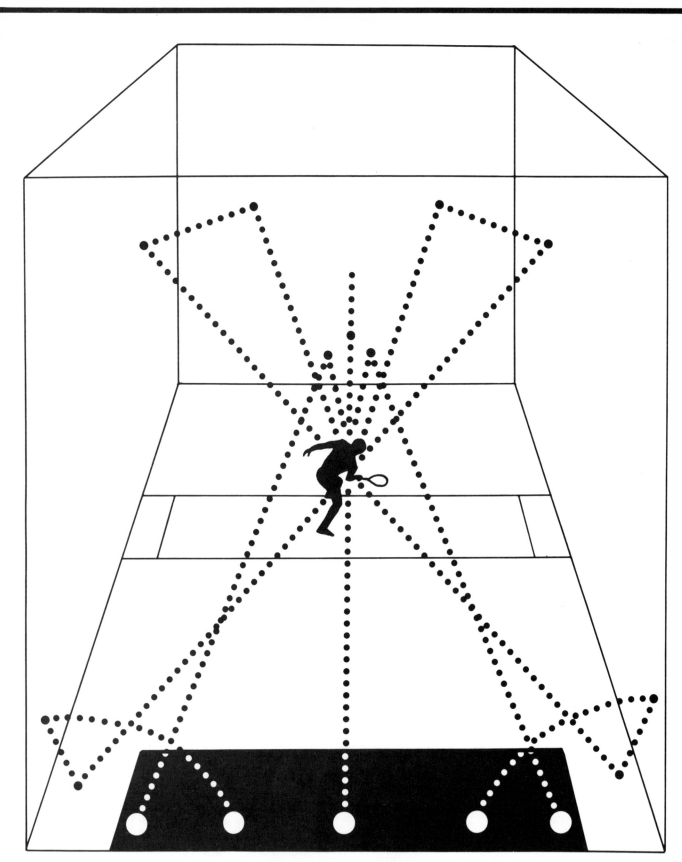

The "Imaginary Rectangle"

Chapter 4

Fundamentals of Serving

There is no weapon in racquetball that is more important than the serve. As the server, you control the game. By the proper selection, placement, and execution of the serving stroke, you keep your opponent on the defensive. He can only react to your strategy. You have plenty of time to plan what you're going to do. You have plenty of room in which to execute your plan.

Equally important, you, as the server, are the only one who can score a point. Your opponent may pull off a spectacular kill or an artfull passing shot, but it won't earn him anything more than the opportunity to step into the service zone.

Concentration is a key element in successful serving. The fact that you have two chances to make a good serve should not entice you to relax. Every first serve that goes long, short, or takes a three-wall carom removes the tactical advantages you enjoy as the server and hands them to your opponent. Try to think in terms of having 21 serves result in 21 points.

There are four basic serves—the low drive, the half lob, the Z, and the high lob. On each one, your goal should be to serve the ball into one of the back corners so that it takes its second bounce within an imaginary rectangle that extends 5 feet forward of the back wall and 3 feet from each of the side walls. When you're able to place the ball within this area, it makes it difficult for your opponent to muster an effective return, and you also give yourself the opportunity to get repositioned at center court.

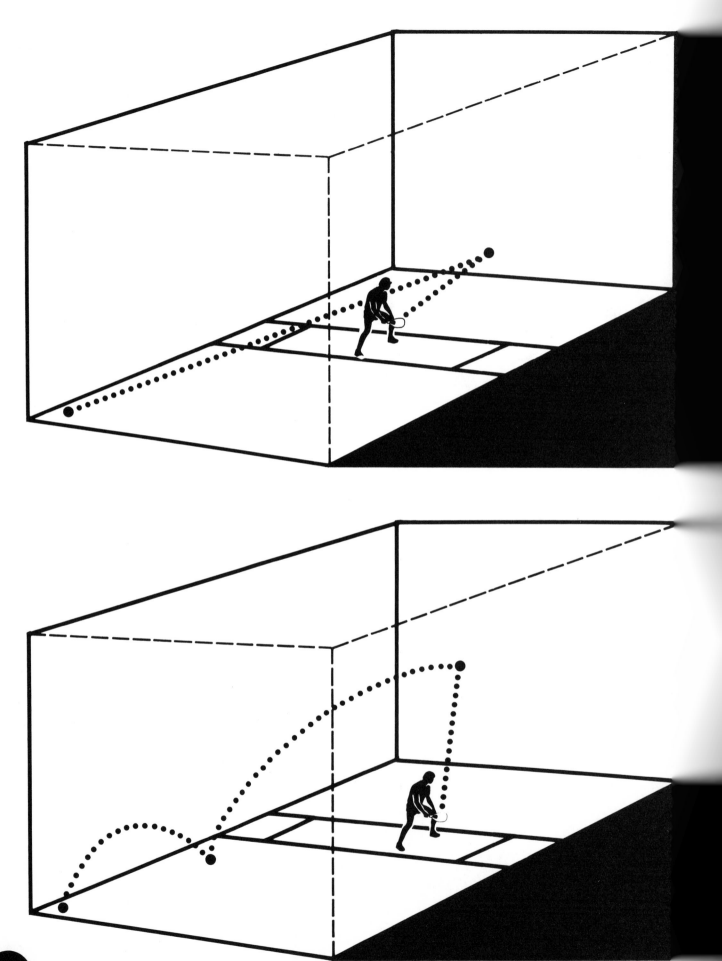

The Low-drive Serve

Also called the power drive, this is racquetball's bread-and-butter serve, especially among power hitters. The low-drive can keep your opponent "leaning" in anticipation of where it's going to go, thus making him vulnerable to a change-of-pace stroke or balls hit into the opposite corner.

Serve from the center of the court. Hit hard with a wrist-popping forehand stroke, driving the ball for a spot about knee high and to the left of center on the front wall.

You want the ball to skip as low as possible into the back corner. Ideally, it will die or roll feebly off the side wall.

It's vital that you don't allow the ball to rebound directly off the back wall. Doing so can give your opponent an easy return. To prevent this from happening, keep the ball low. (After all, it's called the *low*-drive serve.) It must hit the front wall at a point within 3 feet of the floor.

The Half-lob Serve

This is a change-of-pace serve, used when you feel your opponent is getting used to your low drives. When properly hit, the half-lob serve strikes the front wall, rebounds 2 or 3 feet beyond the service line, and then carries deep toward the back corner. Your opponent is likely to be forced to contact the ball at around shoulder level, which may result in a return that caroms off the ceiling.

The half-lob can be served from the center or either side of the service zone. There's no powerful swing, no wrist snap.

Concentrate on direction. As you swing through, keep your elbow bent slightly and firm up your wrist. It's similar to a tennis stroke. But you have to disguise what you're doing. If your opponent figures out in advance what you're up to, he can rush forward and cut off the ball with the idea of executing a kill or passing shot.

Besides its use in changing the game's pace, the half-lob has value as a second serve, since it's easier to be accurate with it than with any of the other serves.

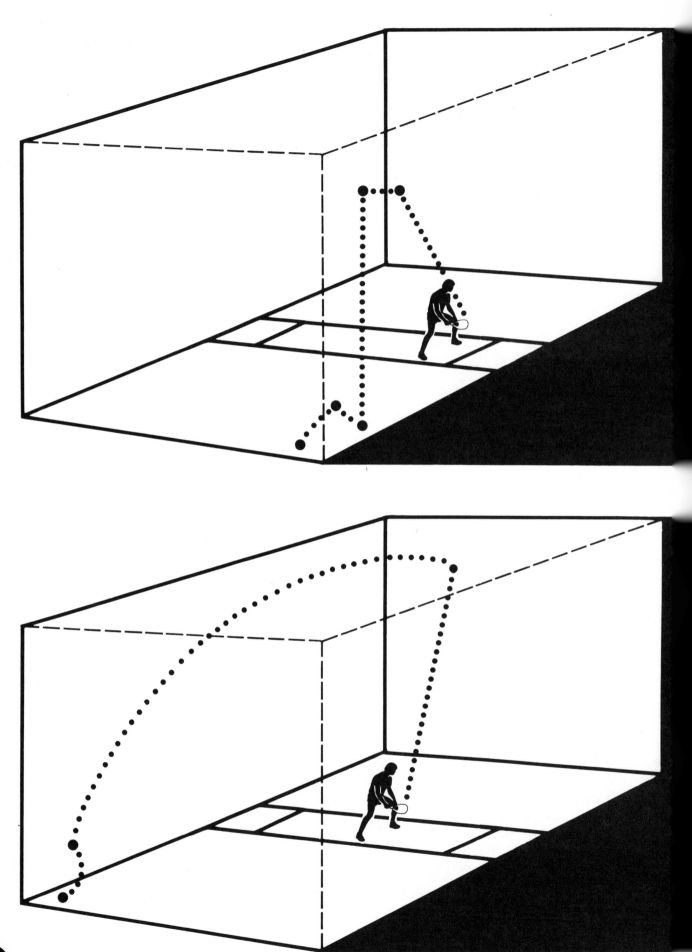

The Z Serve

Many players fail to consider the Z as a basic serve. Yet when properly executed, it can be very troublesome to your opponent, especially in the back corners of the court.

Its name is derived, of course, from the Z-shaped pattern the ball takes. It should strike the front wall about 5 or 6 feet from the floor and at a distance of 9 to 12 inches from the corner. It caroms to the side wall, then rebounds diagonally across the court, striking the floor before hitting the opposite wall.

The Z can be served either from the extreme right side or the extreme left side of the service zone. You need a good wrist snap for it to be effective.

The principal reason that many players shun the Z serve is because it seems complicated, what with all the crazy rebounding the ball does. But the basic laws of physics are in control. If you're accurate with your shot and have the right velocity, the carom-ing that follows is as automatic as the working of gravity.

But you must be accurate. If you hit the front wall at too great a distance from the corner (more than 12 inches), the ball will ricochet into the back wall, setting up an easy return for your opponent. Or if you get too close to the corner (less than 9 inches), the ball will rebound off the opposite side wall, again providing your opponent with an easy setup.

You also have to be sure to get sufficient height into your shot. While the usual recommended target is 5 to 6 feet above the floor, some top-flight players suggest 10 to 12 feet. Practice will enable you to find the target that yields the best Z pattern.

Some players use the Z in an ace attempt. But usually, because it depends more on accuracy than on velocity, it is used as a second serve.

The High-lob Serve

The high-lob serve is executed in much the same manner as the half-lob serve—with the elbow slightly bent and the wrist firm. The emphasis is on accuracy, not velocity. Again, you must disguise what you're planning to do.

The ideal high-lob serve strikes the front wall near the ceiling and rebounds toward the back corner, brushing the side wall before hitting the floor and dying. You have to be right on target. A high-lob that fails to hit the side wall, rebounding directly to the back wall, is likely to mean trouble for you. It gives the receiver an easy bounce and plenty of time to get set.

Chapter 5
The Service Return

Anytime you're receiving a serve, you're on the defensive. You're positioned in the back court instead of at center court. You have no chance to score. An effective service return is the best way to gain the initiative.

The usual position for returning a serve is midway between the side walls and from 2 to 4 feet from the back wall. Face the server in a ready position, your feet about shoulder-width apart. Lean forward from the waist. Hold your racquet in front of your body at about knee level. Get up on your toes so you're ready to move in any direction.

The rules governing service returns state:

· When the ball is being served, you must stand at least 5 feet behind the short line.

· You cannot return the ball until it has passed the short line.

· You are permitted to return the ball before it touches the floor—that is, "on the fly." You *must* return it before it touches the floor twice.

· Your return must send the ball to the front wall, but it can hit either of the side walls or the ceiling first. It cannot, however, come in contact with the floor before hitting the front wall.

Whenever possible, be the aggressor when returning serves. Use your drives to send your opponent forward or force him to the sides. Your ceiling balls should drive him back toward the corners.

When your opponent serves a low drive, step into the ball and slam it back as quickly as possible. You don't want to give him time to set up. If the ball should pop high into the air, let it carom off the back wall before you drive it back.

In the case of a lob serve that is high and losing speed fast, dart forward and hit it before it bounces near the short line, or hit it immediately after it bounces. You don't want to allow the ball to bounce over your head. If, on the other hand, the lob is high but is not losing velocity, let it rebound off the back wall. Then you should have an opportunity for a kill return.

To return a Z serve, try to make contact just before or just after it brushes the side wall. Don't wait to see whether it's going to ricochet off the back wall. It's likely to die before it gets there.

Top-rated players recognize these basic returns—the cross-court pass, the kill shot, and the ceiling ball.

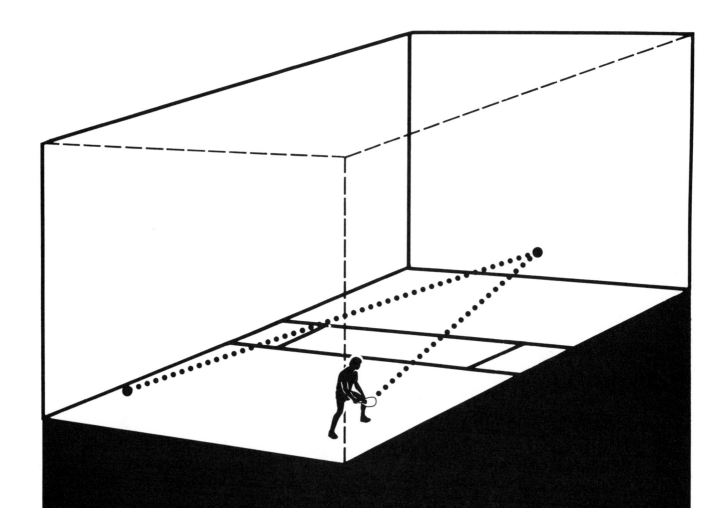

The Cross-court Pass

The safest of the returns, the cross-court pass should be targeted toward the center of the front wall, the idea being to drive the ball past your opponent who is stationed at center court. Ideally, the cross-court pass forces your opponent into the back court to make the return. When that happens, shoot forward and into position to launch an attack. Cross-court passing shots that are low, hard, and beyond the opponent's reach are almost impossible to return effectively.

If you're not sure you can put the ball beyond the opponent's reach, keep it as low as possible and reduce the angle. In other words, blast the ball into the wall so it rebounds right at him. This can be a tough shot to handle—in fact, there are times when you'll be able to handcuff an opponent totally with this strategy.

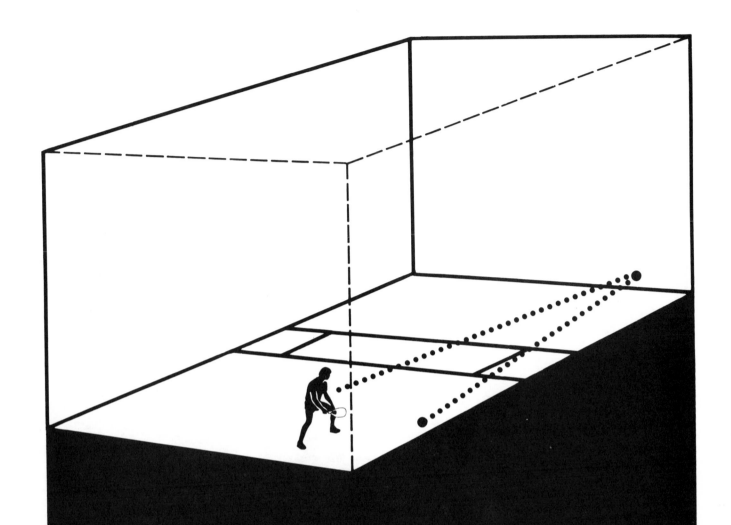

The Kill Shot

This is more risky than the cross-court passing shot, and it should be used only when you are reasonably sure it's going to be successful. The ball hits low on the front wall and caroms away with so little bounce that it's impossible to return. But realize that your opponent has better court position than in the case of the cross-court pass, and thus if the ball doesn't roll out, he has an easy return.

A variation of this kill shot is the down-the-wall pass. After rebounding off the front wall, the ball travels close to the side wall and into the back court and dies before hitting the back wall.

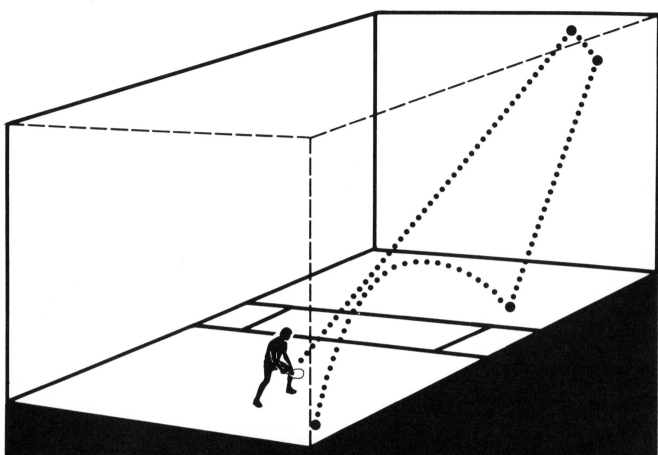

The Ceiling Ball

Of all the service returns, the ceiling ball is the most difficult to make. Nevertheless, you should consider it a vital part of your repertoire. In fact, an axiom of racquetball is: "When in doubt, go for the ceiling."

As this may suggest, the ceiling return is defensive in nature. Use it whenever you want to "buy" some time. It gives you a chance to catch your breath and get set for the next shot.

When executing the shot, go for a ceiling target that is 2 to 3 feet in front of the front wall. The ball should carom to the front wall, to the floor, and then rebound toward your opponent's backhand corner. When properly hit, a ceiling ball will send your opponent scrambling back to get into position, and he's likely to end up alongside you.

Getting the right velocity is important. If you hit with too much power, the ball is likely to rebound off the back wall. Do the opposite—hit too softly—and your opponent can rush in and smash a low drive off the rebound.

Remember, you must pick your shots when using this shot. If you find yourself hitting ceiling returns frequently, it can mean you've developed a negative attitude; you've become defensive-minded. You can't score points unless you take over the serve, and that means you must start playing aggressively.

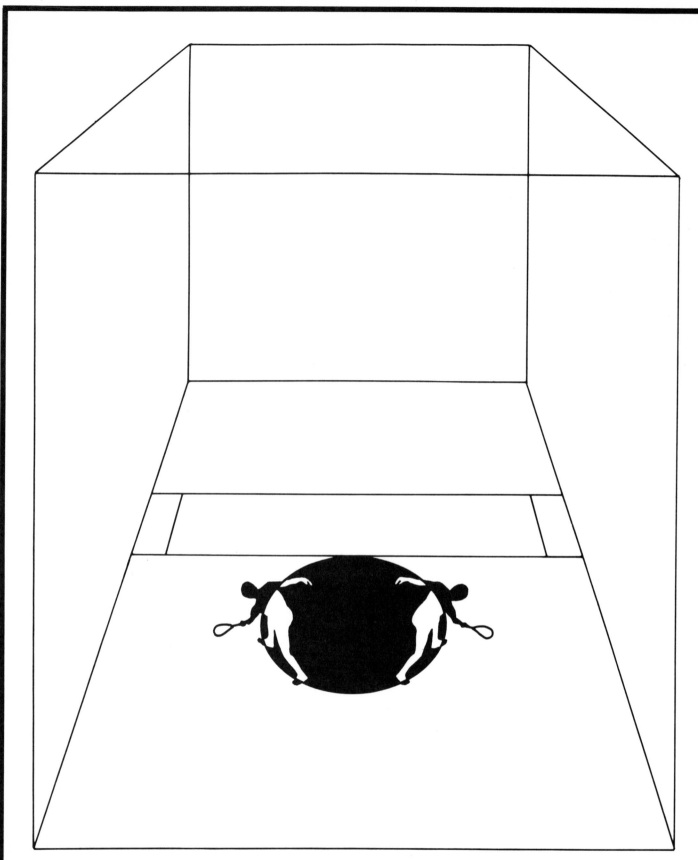

The "Magic Circle"

Chapter 6
Rallying

To win points consistently in racquetball, you must maintain a dominant center-court position. In specific terms, the best place to be during a rally is within the "magic circle," an imaginary circle that is 7 feet in diameter, with its center 3.5 feet behind the short line. When the ball is on the right side of the court, you should position yourself more toward the circle's right edge. When play moves to the left, you move left, again keeping within the circle's perimeter. This strategy enables you to anticipate your opponent's kill attempts in the corner of his passing shots along the side walls. If he attempts a cross-court pass, you have an additional split second to get into position to cover the shot.

Serving Strategy

Let's assume you are the server. Throughout the rally, you must work diligently to maintain your center-court dominance. This means you must keep both your opponent and your own shots out of the center area. Try to force your opponent to shoot down the middle.

When you serve, it's usually best to stand in the center of the service zone. This gives you the best angles to the back corners and the greatest number of service options. Never serve down the middle.

Learn to anticipate the return. After serving, backpedal to a position just behind the short line and step to the side to which you've served, always keeping your upper body parallel to the front wall. Turn your head slightly so you can glance at your opponent as he moves to make the return.

Receiving the Serve

Your basic strategy when you're the receiver should be to hit a return that will force your opponent out of center court. Then you rush up and take over that position.

Take your stance in the center of the court, about two steps in from the back wall. This enables you to get to either corner quickly. When the ball caroms off the front wall, try to step forward and into the ball when executing your shot.

Whether you're receiving or serving, and you're unsure of what to do in a given situation, the best strategy usually is to slam the ball at the front wall as low and as hard as possible. If it's low enough and hard enough, the shot will put your opponent on the defensive. He'll be forced to execute a quick and desperate return that can lead to a kill shot on your part. Or he even may be handcuffed completely and forced into an outright error.

The Kill Shot

Once a rally gets going, your goal should be to go for a kill shot at every reasonable opportunity, thus ending the rally or at least drawing a weak return from your opponent. The words "at every reasonable opportunity" are very important. A kill usually is a gamble. If the shot goes awry, you'll probably end up losing your serve or handing your opponent a point. But when you're facing an opponent at about the same level of ability as yours, kill shots are the only certain way in which you can come out a winner.

Even players of limited experience quickly come to recognize kill-shot opportunities. It's obvious that when you are in center court and your opponent is behind you, a chance for a kill shot arises. Or should your opponent be positioned at about midcourt and move to the right, you have the chance to kill the ball on the left side. Another opportunity presents itself when the ball rebounds off the back wall and into your hitting range.

After each kill attempt, strive to regain your center-court position. If the kill fails, you'll then be less vulnerable than you otherwise might be to whatever your opponent attempts.

Better players recognize several different types of kill shots. The paragraphs that follow describe them.

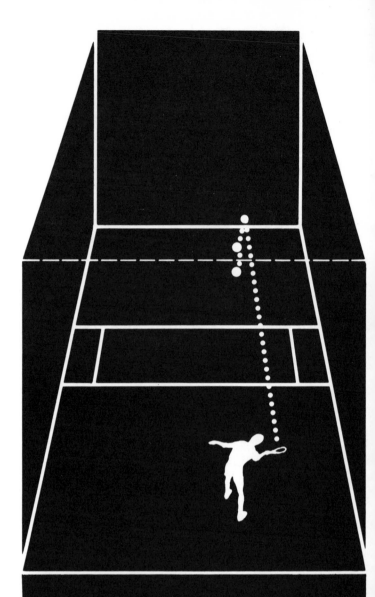

The straight kill

This is the shot you should use in 60 to 70 percent of your kill attempts. It's a ball that's hit straight and low into the front wall, takes two quick bounces, then dies before your opponent has a chance to reach it. Since the ball strikes only one surface, there's little chance of anything going wrong.

The roll-out

This is the perfect kill shot. After it hits the front wall, the ball rebounds to roll along the floor. Even if your opponent happens to be in a position for the return, he'll find the roll-out unhittable.

The pinch shot

Used to best advantage when your opponent is behind you or off to one side, the pinch shot hits low and tight in one of the front corners, then dies. By the time your opponent reacts to the shot hitting the side wall, it's too late for him to retrieve the ball at the front wall.

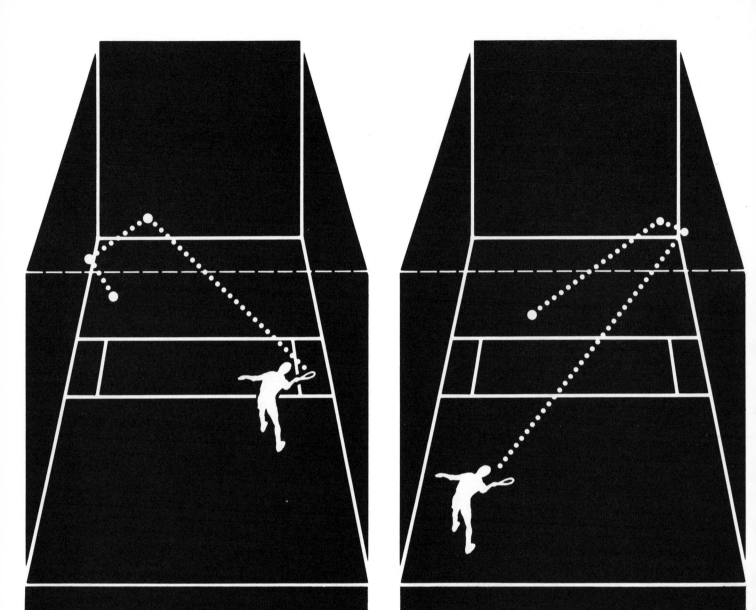

From front wall to side wall

This is more risky than the pinch shot and should be used only when your opponent is fairly deep in the back court. The problem is that should the shot be poorly directed or hit with too much power, it can rebound toward center court. To prevent this from happening, attempt the shot on the left side of the court only when you happen to be positioned on that side (or on the right side only when you're stationed on the right). Keep it low. Try to get the ball merely to brush the wall. Then it will be virtually unreturnable.

The overhead kill

Hitting down, making contact at about the level of your head, slam the ball directly into one of the front corners.

66

Use the kill shot whenever a scoring opportunity presents itself, but passing shots—those that rebound beyond your opponent's reach—are important, too. They add variety to your attack and help to keep him off balance. The more often you drive the ball down a wall or send it cross-court (without permitting it to ricochet off the back wall), the greater your chances of maintaining center-court dominance. You're making your opponent increase his range of coverage and reducing his ability to execute clear-cut kills.

Try to use the entire court whenever you attempt to pass, choosing a shot that puts the ball as far as possible from your opponent. Even if the pass doesn't result in earning you a point or the serve, at least you'll get your opponent out of position.

There are two basic types of passing shots: the cross-court pass and the down-the-wall pass.

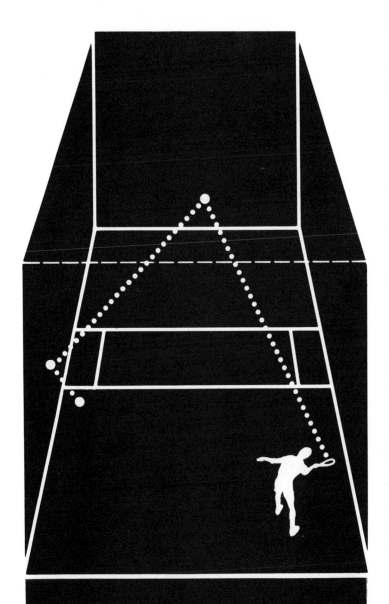

Cross-court pass

Use this pass when your opponent is in front court or in center court. Your target is the center of the front wall. The ball traces a V pattern. If you miss your target, there's a chance the ball will rebound off the side wall and into center court. Ideally, the ball should hit the side wall near the short line, then ricochet toward the opposite back corner.

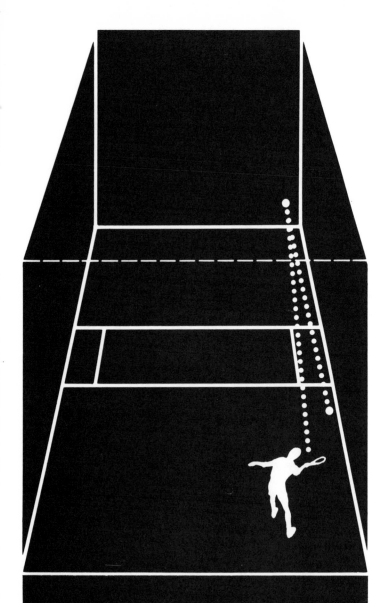

Ceiling shots

The closer you are to the back wall, the more remote the possibility of your executing a successful kill or a passing shot. If you find yourself deep in the back court, your opponent in front of you, your best shot is probably a ceiling shot.

Aim for a target on the ceiling that is about 4 to 5 feet from the front wall. The ball then will carom into the front wall, take a high bounce in the vicinity of the service zone and continue toward the back wall. Angle the shot toward your opponent's backhand corner.

A ceiling ball will force your opponent to vacate center court and cope with a ball that may be as high as his head or even higher. It's not an easy shot to return effectively.

If your accuracy is not your strong suit and you feel you're going to be off target, be certain at least to hit the ceiling. Even if you hit several feet in front of the recommended ceiling target (a point 4 to 5 feet from the wall), the ball still will carry deep after rebounding. But if you miss the ceiling completely, sending the ball directly to the front wall, it's going to carom to the back wall after bouncing somewhere around midcourt, giving your opponent the chance for a kill return.

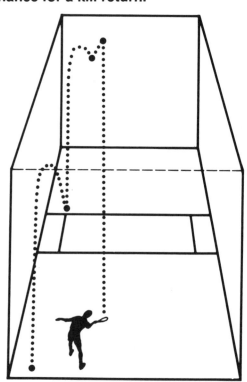

Down-the-wall pass

Hit the ball so it rebounds from the front wall at a shallow angle so it remains close to the side wall as it travels. Be sure to keep the ball low; otherwise it can rebound all the way to the back wall. And be sure it doesn't kick off the side wall, unless it makes contact behind your opponent. You want to hit a ball that hits deep in the back court, then dies.

The Overhead

The overhead is an alternative to the ceiling shot, used to change the pace of a rally. For example, it's a good shot to use when you're being forced into the back court by a high, bouncing ball and don't wish to slow down the rally with a ceiling shot.

But the overhead shot is not easy to execute. Some players compare it to the motion you use in throwing a baseball; others say it resembles the overhead stroke common to tennis or badminton. Use a forehand grip and face sideways as the ball comes toward you. Begin the racquet's swing from a point behind your right shoulder. Straighten your arm and cock your wrist as you swing. Shift your weight to your front foot. Your arm straightens and your wrist uncocks as you make contact. The point of contact is about a foot in front of your shoulder and above the level of your head. Be sure to follow through.

When you plan to execute the overhead drive from a position in the deep back court, aim for the front wall at a point 3 or 4 feet above the floor. Either angle the shot so it travels parallel to a side wall into the back corner, or slam it straight into the front wall so it rebounds fast and hard at your opponent's body. Be careful about hitting with too much power, a mistake that can easily drive the ball into the back wall.

There is also an overhead kill, but it's very risky. It's an overhead that you hit straight and low into the front wall. It takes two bounces and dies before your opponent can get to it. You have to disguise your intention when you're moving to hit, making your opponent think you're going to unleash an overhead drive.

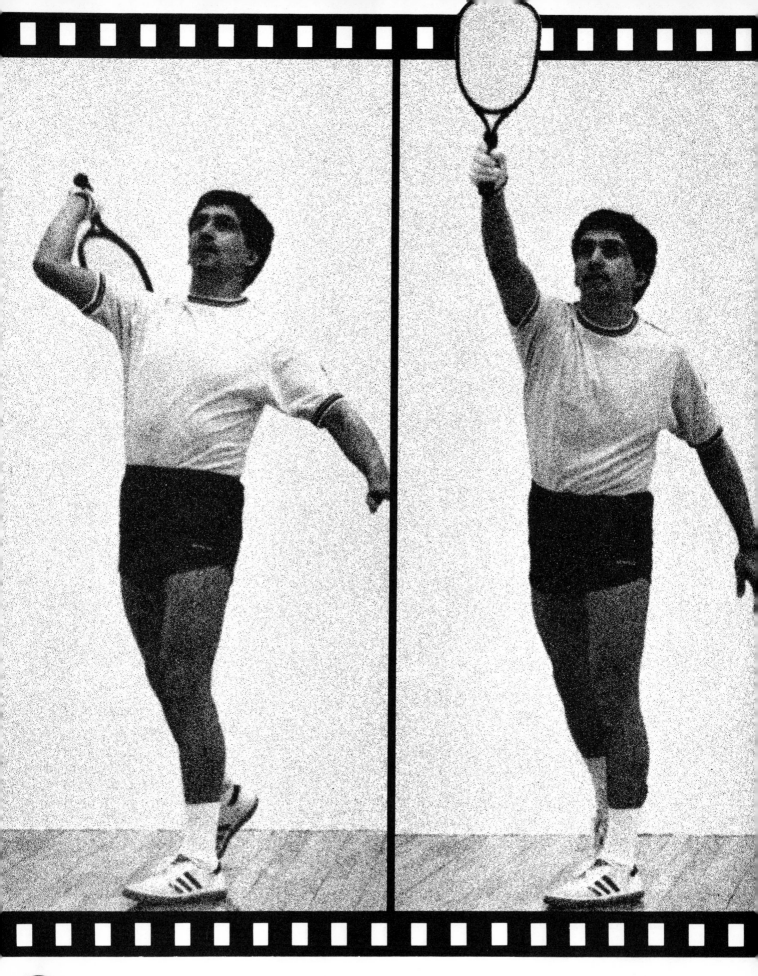

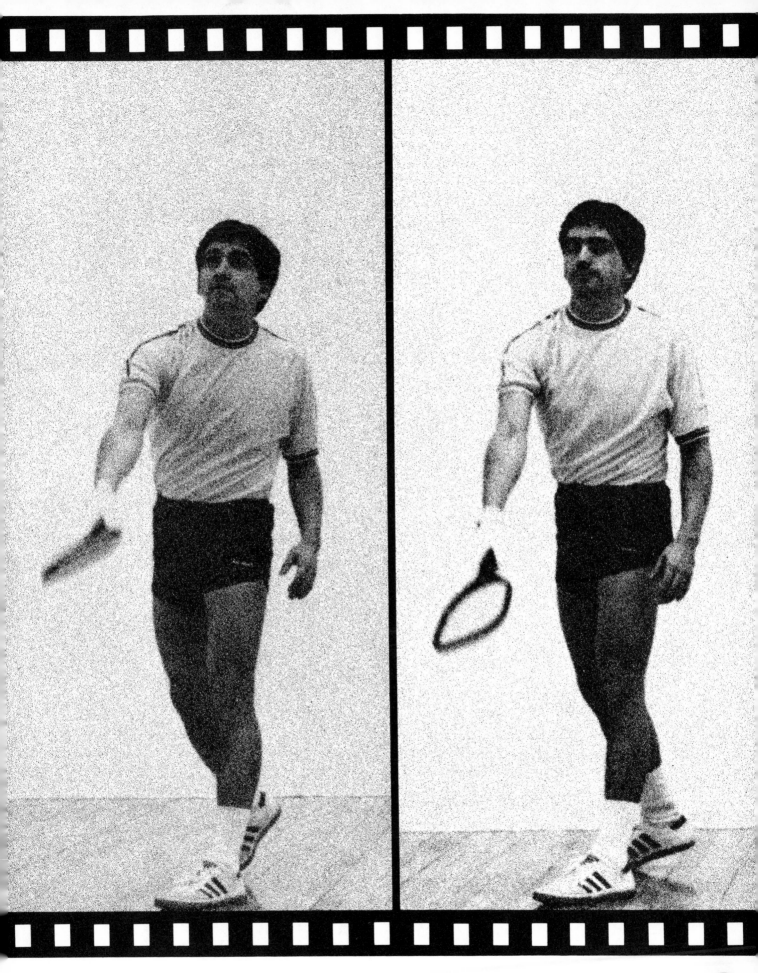

1

2

3

4

5

6

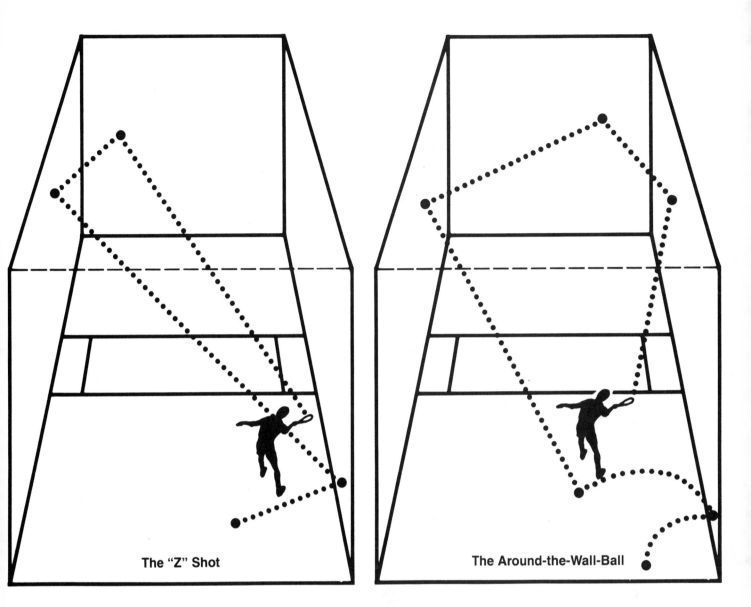

The "Z" Shot

The Around-the-Wall-Ball

The Z Shot

When you're under pressure and feel like slowing things down but you're unable to hit a ceiling ball, the Z may be the shot for you to use. It hits the front wall first, caroms to the side wall, ricochets to the opposite side wall, making contact at a point about 4 or 5 feet from the back wall. Last, the ball ricochets off the side wall, traveling in a path that's almost parallel to the back wall. As you've probably figured out, the shot's path has generally the same configuration as the twenty-sixth letter of the alphabet.

The Z ball can be troublesome for your opponent if he's not used to coping with shots that angle sideways. Also, since he's very close to the back wall, his swing may be restricted. But these hardships can be overcome by a canny player, which means you should not employ the Z shot with any frequency.

A variation of the Z is the around-the-wall ball. Like the Z, it is a change-of-pace shot. With the Z, you target on the front wall, but in the case of the around-the-wall ball, you go for the side wall, aiming for a point about 3 feet from the corner. The ball ricochets into the front wall, travels cross-court into the opposite side wall, then rebounds on a diagonal path toward the back corner, bouncing at a point about midway between the short line and the back wall and caroming into the back wall. You've probably hit a good many around-the-wall balls by accident. It's an alternative shot to use when you're seeking to "buy" time and you're not in a position to hit a ceiling shot. But it has the drawback of being relatively easy to cut off. A canny opponent can dart forward and kill the ball before it bounces.

73

Chapter 7
Strategy and Tactics

Once you're armed with the knowledge of how to execute the basic strokes, you've mastered the art of serving, and you know when to pass and when to kill, you may feel supremely confident. But the confidence is likely to last only until you find yourself facing a player of skill and experience. The ball starts caroming over your head; it clings to the side walls and takes weird bounces on the back corners. You may feel as if you're involved in a game you know nothing about. If this happens to you, don't become a racquetball dropout. Before very long, you'll find you'll be able to read the ball and anticipate the path it's going to take. This chapter is meant to help.

Covering Serves

Trying to cope with the low, hard drives or searing Z's from the racquet of a skilled server is no easy task. At times it may be difficult to manage even a weak return.

But there are a number of things you can do to tip the scales in your favor. First of all, check your stance. You should be about a full stride from the back wall. Your weight should be evenly distributed so you can explode away either to the right or to the left. Hold your racquet with a backhand grip, since the majority of serves are going to go to your backhand side. Watch the server carefully, trying to figure out what type of ball he's going to hit and where he's going to place it.

When you can get to the ball in time to set up properly, drive it into the nearest front corner on a kill attempt or try a down-the-wall passing shot. Either of these can force your opponent out of center court.

Less risky is the cross-court pass. You're likely to have much more of the court to hit into when you're confronted by your opponent's return.

When your opponent serves a half lob that you're unable to cut off and the ball doesn't have the legs to reach the back wall, a ceiling ball probably is your best bet. A Z shot into the far corner is another possibility.

Always keep your overall strategy in mind. You want your returns to force your opponent forward or to either side. You want to be the one who occupies center court.

Good returns depend on the ability to react instinctively and on a powerful stroke. On the forehand side, you want to get your entire body into the swing whenever possible. On both forehands and backhands, you need plenty of wrist snap. Poorly executed shots lead to your opponent's easy putaways.

Cutting Off the Ball

Your opponent has sent a low drive to the front wall, and the ball comes rocketing toward you at about knee level. Should you cut it off or let it continue to the back wall? That's a question you'll have to answer countless times during a game.

A rule of thumb established by top-flight players can be helpful. It states: Swing at any ball that comes to you at waist level or below. (Thus, in the case above, you'd swing away.)

There are exceptions, however. If you're not well set up, and if you know that any ball you hit is going to result in an offensive return, let the ball go to the wall and take your chances there. In other words, if you don't have a chance for an outright kill or you're not certain you're at least going to be putting pressure on your opponent, there's no advantage in trying to cut off the ball. You don't want to hit the ball just for the sake of hitting it. That's not playing aggressively. Eventually you'll give your opponent a shot he can convert into a winner.

Back-wall Play

To the advanced player, a ball that caroms off the back wall is a gift, an easy setup. For some beginners, however, a ball that rebounds off the back wall creates panic. It shouldn't; back-wall shots are easy to cope with once you understand how to get into position. The shot itself is a simple, full-forward stroke.

There are two types of back-wall situations. One results from a shot that travels on a direct path from the front wall to the back wall, rebounding somewhere near the midcourt area. The other results from a shot that comes off the ceiling to the back wall, the direct result of a ceiling shot that has been hit with too much power and targeted too close to the front wall.

In handling either ball, getting good position is the key. Beginners usually make the mistake of setting up too far in front of the ball. As they get set to swing, they suddenly realize that the ball is behind them. They then have to reach out fast to make the return. They fail to hit the ball squarely as a result.

The trick is to place yourself *behind* the point where you judge the ball is going to bounce. Then you simply shuffle forward into the ball. In other words, you should always be moving forward on these shots, never back. Moving forward enables you to

hit with power and accuracy.

Practice this shot by standing in the back court about 5 feet from the back wall. Face the side wall to your right. Toss the ball into the back wall with an underhand motion, releasing it about head high. Toss it hard enough so it will rebound near your feet. As it rebounds and begins to rise, shuffle your feet toward the front wall, swing, and hit.

As your timing and footwork improve, make the drill more challenging. Hit the ball into the front wall, allowing it to rebound off the front wall. Next, hit the ball into the front wall so it caroms into a side wall before rebounding off the back wall.

The back-wall shot following a hard ceiling return is more of a problem. The ball descends off the wall instead of rebounding away from it. As a result, you have less time to get into position. Make a judgment as to where the ball is going to land, then quickly set up behind that point. But in this case, you must set up even farther back, perhaps going all the way to the wall. Then simply shuffle forward until the ball is in your hitting zone, and swing away.

To practice the back-wall shot off a ceiling ball, merely hit long, hard ceiling shots. On each, set up well behind the rebound, and shuffle into it.

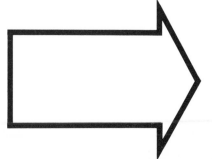

Playing the Back Corners

Since virtually any skilled opponent is going to aim his serves and down-the-wall and cross-court passes into the back corners, it is vital that you become a skilled back-corner player. Not many individuals are. No matter how experienced you become, you'll never be able to anticipate all of the bizarre bounces the ball can take in that part of the court where one wall meets another. And even if you should happen to get a readable bounce, you have to execute your swing in cramped quarters. It's something like swinging a racquet in a telephone booth. No wonder that even a near-miss that caroms into a corner can be a telling shot.

Stay low, bending in the knees, whenever you go into a corner to get the ball. Have your racquet in a ready position. If you do get a chance to swing, your best bet is to go for the ceiling with the ball. If a ceiling shot isn't possible, try flicking the ball toward the front wall with a quick wrist snap. Remember, a weak return is better than no return at all.

Side-wall Play

Most beginners play the side walls incorrectly. Instead of waiting for the rebound, they charge toward the wall, swinging frantically, before they've made any judgment as to the ball's rebound angle or its velocity. Often they mishit the ball as a result and even occasionally fail to hit it at all.

Patience is the key element whenever you're playing a side-wall shot. Keep well away from the wall until the ball makes its carom and you're able to read the rebound angle. Then step into position and swing.

Of course, your racquet has to be in a cocked, ready-to-hit position well before the ball makes contact with the wall.

Try to keep relaxed. Your knees should be well bent and your weight should be forward. You want to be able to adjust your position to the right or left, forward or back, in keeping with any situation that might arise.

You need different strategy when the ball comes straight off the front wall and hugs the side wall, traveling parallel with it as it

heads for the back corner. In such a case you have to step up and swing, practically scraping the ball off the wall. Naturally, there's a psychological barrier you have to overcome, the fear that you're going to swat the wall with your racquet. You can

conquer this fear in practice sessions. Toss a ball to the front wall so it rebounds within a millimeter or so of the side wall, then step toward the wall and swing. You'll get so you can just graze the wall with the racquet.

Chapter 8
Doubles Play

Doubles, a form of play in which two pairs of players oppose each other, is growing in popularity by leaps and bounds. The action is faster than in singles, but it requires less stamina. After all, you are responsible for protecting only one side of the court.

You can choose about anyone for your doubles partner and enjoy the game, but for the greatest success you should seek out an individual whose skills complement your own. If you have a good forehand, look for a partner who is skilled in backhand shots. If power and aggressiveness are hallmarks of your game, your partner should be a strong back-wall player, a defensive specialist. You and your partner should have a full and open discussion of your strengths and weaknesses before you embark on competitive play.

The two of you should develop a system of communicating that can be used during a game. It doesn't have to be complicated. For instance, where there's a question as to which of you should make a return, simply calling out "Yours!" or "Mine!" can decide the issue.

In competitive play, each team is allowed three time-outs during a game, each of which is 30 to 60 seconds in length. Use these periods to discuss game strategy with your partner, deciding upon whatever adjustments might be necessary in light of the game situation.

The shots common to doubles generally are the same as those used in singles. However, there's a greater emphasis on a short, efficient swing in doubles. In the heat of play, its a basic rule of etiquette that each team must give the opposition an open hitting lane for the straight-in-kill, the pinch to the nearest front corner, and a reasonable angle for the cross-court shot.

Basic Formations

Most teams arrange themselves in a side-by-side formation, with each player responsible for half of the court. Each takes up his stance on one side of an imaginary line that extends from the front wall to the back wall, dividing the court in half.

The side-by-side formation works to best advantage when one of the partners has a strong backhand (or is left-handed). This player is responsible for the left side of the court. Usually he stations himself deeper than his teammate, taking up a position about midway between the short line and the back wall. The other player is just behind the short line.

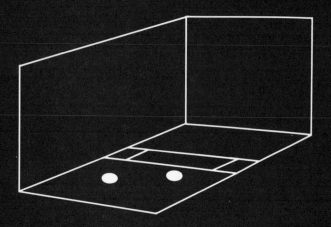

Other teams prefer the I formation, with both players positioning themselves in the center of the court in back of the short service line, one player behind the other. The front player is the quicker, more aggressive player. The player behind has a good ceiling game and is skilled in handling back-court balls.

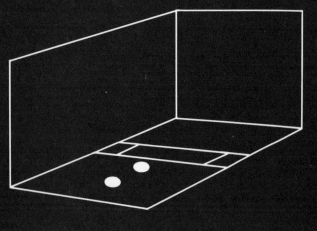

Serving

When a team gets the serve, one partner does the serving. If he loses the serve, the team is out. For the duration of the game, *both* partners serve before the team is out.

When serving, the server stands in the service box, as in singles. His partner stands in the service box, too, and must remain there until the ball has rebounded across the short line.

Usually it's best to take your stance in the center of the service zone and target on the back corner, using the same types of shots as in singles and the same front-wall targets. Always strive to maintain your center-court position. It gives you the greatest opportunity for returning your opponent's shots and, since you're closer to the front wall, enables you to be more accurate.

Avoid sending low drives into the back wall behind your partner. As he moves out of the service box, there is a good chance he'll be struck by the ball. Z serves and high lobs are used more frequently in doubles play than in singles.

Basic Doubles Strategy

Kills are vital to success in doubles. Passes are effective only when your opponents are out of position.

Usually it's a mistake to try to kill the ball when returning the serve—unless you can uncork a roll-out. Your first goal should be to drive the opposition out of center court. If the serve is weak, try a cross-court shot, targeting on the side wall behind one of your opponents. Try driving them into the back court with ceiling and Z shots.

In singles, a rule of thumb states that if the ball comes off the wall toward you and it's at waist level or below, don't allow it to go to the back wall. That rule also applies in doubles.

The overhead drive and overhead kill generally are more effective in doubles than in singles. Rely on ceiling balls when your opponents are in center court and you don't want to risk a kill or a pass.

It's important to keep your eye not only on the ball, but also on your partner. If he happens to get lured out of position, it's up to you to cover for him.

One team usually tries to isolate the better player on the opposition team, sending most of their shots to the weaker opponent. When the stronger opponent relaxes and drops his guard, slap a low drive to his backhand side.

Cutthroat

If you can get only three people together, try a game of cutthroat. The rules are simple. The server competes against the other two players, continuing to serve and score points until he loses a rally. Then a second player gets to serve, then the third. Each player keeps his own score. The first to score 21 points is the winner.

Glossary

ace—A serve that bounces twice before the receiver can return it, resulting in a point for the server.

around-the-wall ball—A defensive shot that goes first to a side wall, then to the front wall, and then rebounds to the other side wall before striking the floor midway between the short line and the back wall.

avoidable hinder—Interference or obstruction, not necessarily intentional, which, in tournament play, results in a loss of serve or point.

back court—The area from the short line to the back wall.

ceiling ball—A shot that hits the ceiling, front wall, and floor before rebounding into the back court.

center court—The area directly behind the service line.

cross-court pass—A shot that travels from one side of the court to the other after hitting the front wall, then heads for the back corner.

cutthroat—A three-player game. When serving, each player competes against and scores points against the other two players. The first player to score 21 points wins.

defensive shot—A shot executed to prolong a rally, not necessarily to win a point.

down-the-wall shot—A shot that rebounds from the front wall to travel close to and parallel to a side wall.

front court—The area between the service line and the front wall.

half-lob serve—A ball hit with medium speed that carries just beyond the back service line and dies before hitting the back wall.

head—The hitting area of the racquet.

high-lob serve—A ball that makes contact with a side wall as it descends into the back court and dies before hitting the back wall.

hitting alley—The lane in which the ball travels on its way to the front wall.

I formation—In doubles play, when one player on a team is stationed in the front court and the other in the back court.

kill—A shot that is unreturnable.

low drive—A hard-hit ball that hits the front wall and then angles toward a back corner.

offensive shot—A shot whose purpose is to win the point or the serve.

overhead—A stroke in which the racquet is brought through from a point behind the shoulder, reaching a level above the server's head.

passing shot—A shot meant to sail into the back court beyond the opponent's reach.

pinch shot—A tight corner shot that hits the front wall first, then the side wall, and then dies.

rally—The exchange of shots between serves.

roll-out—A shot that caroms from the front wall with no bounce, rolling along the floor.

service box—Each of two areas, 18 inches in width, at each end of the service zone, used for serving in doubles.

service zone—The area 5 feet in width and extending to both side walls and from within which the serve must be executed.

short serve—A serve that rebounds off the front wall, then fails to carry beyond the short service line; an illegal serve.

skip ball—A ball that hits the floor before reaching the front wall.

unavoidable hinder—Unintentional interference or obstruction by a player.

Z ball—A shot that hits high on the front wall, caroms to the side wall, then travels to the opposite side wall before striking the floor.

Racquetball Organizations

International Professional
Racquetball Organization
2714 Union Avenue Extension
Memphis, TN 38112

International Racquetball Association
5545 Murray Avenue
Memphis, TN 38104

National Court Clubs Association
423 Central Avenue
Northfield, IL 60093

National Racquetball Club
4101 Dempster Street
Skokie, IL 60076

United States Racquetball Association
4101 Dempster Street
Skokie, IL 60076